101 Recipes Every Teen Needs To Cook

Quick & Easy Favorite Meals Everyone Will Adore (with Fun Tips & Facts)

Isabella Miller

CONTENTS

INTRODUCTION

Hello there, culinary explorers! Welcome to "101 Recipes Every Teen Needs To Cook" where your culinary journey begins. This book isn't just about cooking; it's about embarking on an adventure in your very own kitchen. As a teen, diving into a cookbook of 101 classic favorite recipes is not just about learning to cook; it's a gateway to independence and a journey of self-discovery. Imagine the freedom of creating your own meals, exploring the rich tapestry of everyday favourites, and taking control of your own nutrition and satisfaction.

Cooking is a creative adventure, allowing you to experiment with flavors, adapt dishes to your own taste, and even develop unique creations. It's a practical way to learn life skills like time management and multitasking, all while engaging in a fun and enjoyable activity. Plus, the satisfaction and confidence you gain from preparing and sharing a delicious meal with friends and family is unparalleled. Or just invite them over to cook with you.

This cookbook is more than a collection of recipes; it's a stepping stone into understanding how are favorite, everyday meals are created, and it's a great way to enhance your social skills. Whether you're looking to impress your peers or simply want yo enjoy your favorites at any time, cooked by you. this cookbook is your perfect companion. So, gear up for a delightful culinary journey that promises to spice up your teenage years and equip you with skills that last forever.

HOW TO START?

THE KITCHEN SETUP - YOUR CULINARY PLAYGROUND

Welcome to the heart of your culinary adventure – your kitchen! Start by organizing your kitchen into zones: one for prep, one for cooking, and one for cleaning. Keep your tools and ingredients within easy reach, and you'll be all set to cook up a storm!

ESSENTIAL TOOLS - THE SECRET TO YOUR SUCCESS

Every teen chef needs the right tools to make magic in the kitchen. Begin with the basics: a good chef's knife (watch those fingers!), a cutting board (one for veggies and one for meats), mixing bowls, measuring cups and spoons, and a set of spatulas, whisks and spoons. These are your culinary weapons, and they'll help you tackle most recipes. And remember, you don't need every gadget under the sun – start simple and build your collection as you grow your skills.

MUST-HAVE EQUIPMENT - COOKING MADE EASY

Now, let's talk equipment. A reliable frying pan, a large pot for boiling pasta or making soups, a baking sheet, a blender, and a casserole dish should top your list. With these in your arsenal, you can fry, boil, bake, and roast almost anything.

FRESH INGREDIENTS - THE KEY TO TASTY MEALS

Fresh ingredients bring life to any dish. Always try to have fresh veggies and fruits, dairy (like milk, cheese, and yogurt), and proteins (like chicken, fish, or tofu) on hand. They're not just nutritious but also add color, texture, and flavor to your meals. Remember, the fresher the ingredients, the tastier the dish!

SAFETY AND CLEANLINESS - YOUR KITCHEN MANTRAS

Last but definitely not least, let's talk safety and cleanliness. Always wash your hands before and after handling food. Keep your kitchen clean as you cook – it's not just about hygiene, it makes cooking more enjoyable and manageable. And learn how to handle knives and hot pots safely – no dish is worth a trip to the emergency room!

By following these steps, you'll have a well-equipped, safe, and efficient kitchen ready for all your culinary explorations! Enjoy the journey of becoming a proficient cook within days.

SEVEN ESSENTIAL KITCHEN SKILLS FOR TEENS

1. **Knife Handling:** Grip the knife firmly with your dominant hand, like a handshake, ensuring control and safety. Always cut on a flat surface.

2. **Slicing:** Cut across the food's grain into thin, even slices using the full blade length, with no downward pressure.

3. **Chopping and Dicing**: Use a chef's knife for cutting food into pieces, with chopping for larger pieces and dicing for smaller ones.

4. **Measuring**: Accurate measuring is crucial. Use leveled cups or spoons for dry ingredients and a graduated cup for liquids. Measure dry ingredients before wet ones.

5. **Mixing**: For consistent texture and flavor, mix dry and wet ingredients separately before combining them.

6. **Stirring**: Stir ingredients on a stove to ensure even cooking. Stir continuously to thicken liquids, stir frequently for adding solids to liquids, and stir occasionally to maintain even heat.

7. **Tossing**: Gently lift and flip food in a bowl or pan for even coating or mixing.

KITCHEN TERMINOLOGY

Understand common cooking terms like beating, blending, chilling, cooling, drizzling, folding, greasing, marinating, preheating, puréeing, sautéing, searing, seasoning, simmering, and whisking.

MICROWAVE COOKING TIPS

In a microwave, arrange food for even cooking, flip meats or potatoes midway, and allow a rest time after cooking for heat to disperse evenly.

MAXIMIZING YOUR USE OF POTS AND PANS

In the kitchen, "pans" generally refer to flat cookware like frying pans and baking sheets, ideal for cooking eggs, bacon, pancakes, or baking cookies. "Pots," or saucepans, are deeper and great for making sauces, soups, and boiling pasta. To cook evenly and reduce cooking time, heat your pan slowly for a minute or two before starting. Let pots and pans cool naturally after use; plunging a hot pan into water can cause warping. To prevent boil-overs when cooking pasta or soup, rest a wooden spoon across the pot. Use wooden tools to avoid scratching, especially in nonstick pans. A light spray of nonstick cooking spray in pots and pans can help prevent food from sticking.

CREATIVE AND INTUITIVE COOKING

Feel free to experiment and create your own dishes. Add seasoning throughout cooking and taste as you go, using salt to enhance other flavors. Balance dishes with acids like citrus juices and fats like olive oil.

NAVIGATING THE RECIPES IN THIS BOOK

As you start your cooking journey, refer to the staple ingredients and techniques outlined in this chapter. Each recipe lists needed appliances and is labeled for easy planning. Tips are included for alternative cooking methods or a more convenient cooking. So, are you ready to unleash your inner chef and dive into a world of taste, texture, and tantalizing recipes? Whether you're taking your first steps in cooking or looking to expand your skills, this cookbook is your ultimate guide. Filled with a mix of classic favorites and exciting new dishes, we've designed every recipe to be fun, easy to make, and, of course, super delicious!

And remember, in your kitchen, you're the boss! So, what are you waiting for? Let's heat up those stoves, get our hands messy, and embark on a culinary adventure that'll lead to some lip-smacking creations.

BREAKFAST

Scrambled Eggs

Servings: 1 | **Prep + Cook Time**: 10 minutes

INGREDIENTS

2 tablespoons butter

2 eggs

2 tablespoons milk

¼ teaspoon salt

1/3 teaspoon ground black pepper

DIRECTIONS

1. Crack the eggs into a bowl, add milk, and whisk until well combined. Season with salt and pepper. Melt the butter in a small skillet over medium heat.

2. Add the egg mixture into the skillet and let it sit for a moment, then gently stir with a spatula, allowing the eggs to cook evenly until they are cooked but still moist.

3. Enjoy your tasty scrambled eggs!

TIP

Top with your scrambled eggs with salsa, avocado, or cheese.

FUN FACT

Scrambled eggs is that they were one of the favorite dishes of legendary scientist and inventor, Albert Einstein. It's said that he enjoyed them because of their simplicity. This no-fuss meal allowed him to focus his mental energy on his groundbreaking scientific work. Scrambled eggs, with their humble and straightforward preparation, were a perfect fit for his lifestyle and intellectual pursuits.

Boiled Eggs

Servings: 1 | **Prep + Cook Time**: 15 minutes

INGREDIENTS

2 eggs

Water

DIRECTIONS

1. Place the eggs in a small pot and cover them with cold water by 1 inch.

2. Bring the water to a boil over medium heat, then reduce the heat to low and cover it with a lid.

3. Simmer for 5-6 minutes for soft-boiled and 8-10 minutes for hard-boiled.

4. Fill a bowl with ice water.Transfer the egg to the bowl of ice water using a slotted spoon. Let sit to cool completely.

5. Once cooled, tap the eggs on a hard surface, then roll them gently to loosen the shell. Peel and enjoy!

TIP

Add a pinch of salt to the water when boiling your eggs. This makes peeling them easier.

FUN FACT

If you spin an egg on a flat surface, you can tell if it's boiled or raw just by observing its rotation. A hard-boiled egg will spin smoothly and rapidly, while a raw egg will wobble and spin slowly. This is due to the liquid interior of the raw egg, which doesn't move uniformly, causing an imbalance. On the other hand, the solid interior of a boiled egg allows for a steady, smooth spin

Grilled Ham & Cheese Sandwich

Servings: 1 | **Prep + Cook Time:** 12

INGREDIENTS

1 tablespoon butter

2 sandwich bread slices

2 ham slices

½ cup shredded mozzarella cheese

DIRECTIONS

1. Heat a skillet over medium heat.

2. Brush one side of each bread slice with butter.

3. On one bread slice without butter, place half of the shredded mozzarella cheese.

4. Top with ham slices and then with the remaining mozzarella cheese. Cover with the remaining bread slice, butter-side on top.

5. When the skillet is hot, carefully place the sandwich butter-side down.

6. Cook for about 3 minutes or until the bottom is toasted and golden.

7. Using a spatula, carefully flip the sandwich and toast for another 3 minutes or until the bottom is toasted and golden and the cheese has melted.

TIP

Add a gourmet touch by sprinkling a pinch of freshly chopped basil.

FUN FACT

Known in France as the "Croque Monsieur," this beloved sandwich first appeared on Parisian café menus in 1910. The name "Croque Monsieur" translates to "Mister Crunch," a playful nod to its delightfully crispy exterior. It became an instant classic in French cafes and bistros, known for its combination of toasted bread, creamy melted cheese, and savory ham. This comfort food has since become popular worldwide, and we love it.

Chia Pudding

Servings: 1 | **Prep Time:** 5 minutes + chilling time

INGREDIENTS:

2 tablespoons chia seeds

1/2 cup Greek yogurt

1/2 teaspoon vanilla extract

1 tablespoon honey

6 blueberries for topping

1 tablespoon chopped almonds

DIRECTIONS

1. Combine chia seeds, yogurt, vanilla extract, and honey in a bowl. Stir well to ensure the chia seeds are evenly distributed.

2. Cover the bowl and refrigerate overnight or for at least 4 hours to allow the chia seeds to absorb the liquid and create a pudding-like consistency.

3. Before serving, top with blueberries and add chopped almonds for some extra crunch.

4. Tip: Experiment with different toppings like shredded coconut, chopped hazelnuts, or a dollop of coconut yogurt to add variety and extra flavor to your breakfast pudding.

TIP

Substitute the blueberries for bananas, strawberries, raspeberries, kiwis or other favorite fruits of yours. Subsititute the almonds for walnuts, pecans or hazelnuts.

FUN FACT

Astronauts on space missions enjoy various types of pudding as a part of their meals. Since food in space needs to be non-perishable and easy to consume in zero gravity, pudding is an ideal choice. Imagine floating in space and squeezing a delicious pudding into your mouth – it's like a cosmic experience, while watching the stars.

Cheesy Omelette

Servings: 1 | **Prep + Cook Time**: 10 minutes

INGREDIENTS

2 large eggs

Salt and pepper to taste

½ tablespoon butter

½ tablespoon olive oil

2 tablespoons cheddar cheese, grated

1 teaspoon chopped parsley

DIRECTIONS

1. Crack the eggs into a bowl, add a pinch of salt and pepper, and whisk them together until well combined.

2. Heat a non-stick skillet over medium heat and add butter and olive oil.

3. Pour the whisked eggs into the skillet. Allow the eggs to set slightly at the edges, and then use a spatula to gently lift the edges, letting the uncooked egg flow underneath.

4. Continue lifting and tilting the pan to ensure even cooking. Add shredded cheese on one side of the omelet.

5. Carefully fold the other half of the omelet over the fillings, creating a half-moon shape. Cook for another minute until the omelet is set but still moist inside. Slide the omelet onto a plate and serve immediately.

TIP

Experiment with different fillings like sautéed mushrooms, bell peppers, or onions to customize your omelet.

Traditional Pancakes

Servings: 4 | **Prep + Cook Time:** 15 minutes

INGREDIENTS

¼ cup all-purpose flour

1 tablespoon sugar

1 teaspoon baking powder

1 tablespoon vegetable oil

¼ cup buttermilk

1 egg

1 tablespoon butter, softened

1 cup blueberries

2 tablespoons maple syrup

DIRECTIONS

1. Place the flour, sugar, and baking powder in a medium mixing bowl and stir to combine. Make a small well in the dry ingredients.

2. Combine the oil, buttermilk, and egg in a small mixing bowl and whisk until combined. Pour the wet ingredients into the dry ingredients and stir until just combined. It's okay if the batter is a bit lumpy.

3. Heat a large frying pan over medium heat and lightly grease it with butter. Using a ladle, pour the batter into a 4-inch "puddle" in the pan.

4. Let the pancakes cook until bubbles form on the surface, about 3 minutes. Using a spatula, gently flip the pancakes and cook until golden brown, about 2 minutes more. Repeat with the remaining batter.

5. Serve drizzled with maple syrup and top with blueberries.

TIP

To enhance the flavor, add a dollop of butter and sprinkle with powdered sugar. Accompany with peanut butter or Nutella and enjoy this delightful treat immediately.

Peanut Butter and Jelly Sandwich

Servings: 1 | **Prep Time:** 10 minutes

INGREDIENTS

2 bread slices

2 teaspoons butter

2 tablespoons peanut butter

1-2 tablespoons strawberry jam

DIRECTIONS

1. Heat a skillet to medium-high.

2. Spread butter on one side of each slice of bread. Spread strawberry jam on the other slice of bread.

3. Press the peanut butter and jelly sides together to form a sandwich with the butter on the outside.

4. Cook in the skillet until golden brown, about 2-3 minutes per side.

5. Transfer to a cutting board, cut the sandwich into halves and serve.

TIP

For a twist, use almond butter or other nut butter varieties, and experiment with different fruit jams or fresh fruit such as bananas or strawberries.

FUN FACT

The U.S. military included peanut butter and jelly in their ration packs because they provided a quick source of energy and were easy to carry. Soldiers would mix them together on bread, creating the classic PB&J sandwich we know today. When the soldiers returned home after the war, the popularity of peanut butter and jelly sandwiches skyrocketed, making it a staple in American households and a beloved lunchtime favorite for generations!

Green Smoothie Bowl

Servings: 1 | **Prep Time:** 5 minutes

INGREDIENTS

1 small Granny Smith apple, cored and cut into wedges

1 teaspoon brown sugar, optionally

1 small cucumber, peeled and chopped

2 celery stalks, chopped

2 kale leaves

1 cup baby spinach

2 teaspoons black sesame seeds

DIRECTIONS

1. Place brown sugar, cucumber, celery, kale, spinach, apple, and black sesame seeds in your blender.

2. Puree for 1 minute or until smooth and no large chunks of apple remain.

3. Pour into a bowl and let sit for a few minutes.

TIP

To sweeten the green smoothie, incorporate ripe bananas or dates.

Both are natural sweeteners and blend well in smoothies.

Ripe bananas add a creamy texture and a naturally sweet taste, while dates offer a rich, caramel-like sweetness.

Just a few dates can significantly increase the sweetness of your smoothie.

Remember to pit the dates before blending! For an extra flavor boost, you can also add a splash of vanilla extract.

French Toast

Servings: 1 | **Prep + Cook Time:** 15 minutes

INGREDIENTS

1 egg

4 tablespoons milk

2 thick bread slices

1 tablespoon vegetable oil

1 teaspoon powdered sugar

DIRECTIONS

1. In a small bowl, beat the egg, then add milk and whisk until well blended.

2. Dip the bread slices into the egg mixture and let them soak for 1-2 minutes.

3. Turn the bread one time with a spatula to evenly coat and let it soak for another 3 minutes.

4. Warm the vegetable oil in a large frying pan over medium heat.

5. Add the soaked bread to the frying pan and cook for 6 minutes or until golden brown, flipping the bread once.

6. Sprinkle with powdered sugar. Enjoy!

TIP

Drizzle warm honey over the finished French toast instead of powdered sugar for a honey twist. Garnish with some fresh berries.

FUN FACT

Despite its name, French toast can be traced back to ancient Roman times, long before France was established. The Romans had a dish called "Pan Dulcis," where they would soak bread in a milk and egg mixture and then fry it. The name "French toast" was actually popularized in America. So, this delicious breakfast is a connection to ancient Roman dining tables!

No Time Microwave Granola

Servings: 2 | **Prep + Cook Time:** 5 minutes

INGREDIENTS

2 tablespoons honey

1 ½ tablespoons water

4 teaspoons vegetable oil

¼ teaspoon salt

2/3 cup quick oats

1 tablespoon chopped walnuts

1 tablespoon sesame seeds

2 tablespoons raisins

DIRECTIONS

1. Place the honey, water, vegetable oil, salt, oats, walnuts, and sesame seeds in a microwave-safe bowl and stir.

2. Microwave for 2 minutes on Medium. Stir the mixture and microwave for 1-2 more minutes or until the oats are brown and crisp. Open the microwave and remove the bowl. Add in the raisins and stir to combine.

3. Let the granola cool for 5 minutes before serving.

TIP

You can substitute the oats with muesli. Muesli is an excellent choice it's packed with fiber, whole grains, and essential nutrients to support growth and keep you energized throughout the day.

FUN FACT

A fun fact about granola that's often surprising is that it was actually invented as part of a health movement in the United States in the late 19th century. Dr. James Caleb Jackson, a health food enthusiast and operator of a health spa in New York, created a food called "granula" in 1863. This crunchy cereal was part of the early health food movement and has evolved significantly over the years to become the sweet, tasty, and versatile granola we enjoy today in breakfasts and snacks.

Choco-Peanut Butter Shake

Servings: 1 | **Prep Time**: 5 minutes

INGREDIENTS

1 cup milk

1 teaspoon peanut butter

1 teaspoon chocolate syrup

1 teaspoon maple syrup

1 ripe banana

Ice cubes

DIRECTIONS

1. Pour the milk, peanut butter, chocolate syrup, and maple syrup into a food processor or blender.

2. Add the banana and a handful of ice cubes.

3. Pulse until smooth and creamy.

4. Pour your shake into a glass. Enjoy!

TIP

If the shake is too thick, add more milk; if it's too thin, add more ice.

FUN FACT

The classic American milkshake, is its surprising connection to the invention of the electric blender. Before the blender's invention, milkshakes were hand-shaken and had a much thinner consistency, often just flavored milk. In 1922, a Walgreens employee in Chicago had the idea to add ice cream to the milkshake, which required a more powerful mixing method. This led to the use of the newly invented electric blender, to create the thick, creamy milkshake we know and love today. So, the modern milkshake is not just a treat, but also a product of early 20th-century technological innovation!

Avocado Toast

Servings: 1 | **Prep + Cook Time:** 10 minutes

INGREDIENTS

2 bread slices

1 ripe avocado

Salt and black pepper to taste

2 iceberg lettuce leaves

1 medium tomato, sliced

DIRECTIONS

1. Put the bread slices in your toaster and toast them to your desired doneness.

2. While the bread is toasting, cut the ripe avocado in half, remove the pit, and scoop the flesh into a bowl. Season with the salt and pepper and mash it with a fork.

3. Once the bread is toasted, spread the mashed avocado over the surface.

4. Top the bread slices with lettuce leaves and tomato slices. Enjoy!

TIP

Top your avocado toast with toasted pumpkin seeds or crushed nuts to add a crunch.

FUN FACT

A fun fact about avocado toast is that while it's often considered a modern, trendy dish, its origins can actually be traced back to the early 20th century in California. The region's abundant avocado groves made this fruit a common household staple. According to some food historians, Californians were spreading avocado on bread as early as the 1920s, long before it became a global phenomenon. It's not just a recent hipster creation but a dish with a history and a symbol of contemporary cuisine and healthy eating trends.

Strawberry Muffin In A Mug

Servings: 1 | **Prep + Cook Time:** 10 minutes

INGREDIENTS

1 tablespoon vegetable oil

½ cup flour

2 tablespoons brown sugar

½ teaspoon baking powder

½ cup milk

2 tablespoons strawberries, chopped

½ teaspoon vanilla extract

½ teaspoon lemon zest

Pinch of salt

DIRECTIONS

1. Remove and discard the stems from the strawberries. Cut the strawberries into small pieces.

2. Transfer them to a microwave-safe mug and add all the remaining ingredients. Stir well to combine.

3. Microwave for about 2 minutes or until puffed and cooked. Remove the mug from the microwave and let it sit for 1 minute before eating. Enjoy!

TIP

Before microwaving, place a small piece of chocolate chip into the center of the batter in the mug.

FUN FACT

In some parts of the world, they are used to celebrate birthdays as an alternative to traditional birthday cakes. This is particularly handy for school celebrations where a cake might be too cumbersome. Muffins can be easily customized and decorated with icing, candles, and even written messages, just like a birthday cake. Plus, they offer a convenient, individual serving size, making them a practical choice. So, for those looking for a unique twist on birthday treats, a brightly decorated muffin can be a delightful and personal way to celebrate!

Cinnamon-Apple Oatmeal

Servings: 1 | **Prep + Cook Time**: 10 minutes

INGREDIENTS

1 cup milk

½ cup rolled oats

½ apple, diced

1 teaspoon cinnamon

2 teaspoons brown sugar

Pinch of salt

DIRECTIONS

1. Place the milk, rolled oats, diced apple, cinnamon, brown sugar, and salt in a small microwave-safe bowl.

2. Stir the ingredients together until well combined.

3. Microwave the bowl on high for 2-3 minutes. Keep an eye on it to prevent overflow.

TIP

Top with additional apple slices, a sprinkle of cinnamon, and a handful of chopped almonds for added crunch.

FUN FACT

Did you know that oatmeal is known for its natural soothing and anti-inflammatory properties, making it a popular ingredient in homemade face masks. When combined with fruits like mashed banana or avocado, which are rich in vitamins and antioxidants, the mixture becomes a nourishing treat for the skin. This homemade concoction can help to hydrate, calm, and rejuvenate the skin, leveraging the natural benefits of both oats and fruits. So, fruit oatmeal isn't just a healthy breakfast option; it can also be a part of your natural beauty routine!

Banana Overnight Oats

Servings: 1 | **Prep + Cook Time:** 5 minutes + overnight to chill

INGREDIENTS

1 banana

2 tablespoons chopped walnuts

½ cup old-fashioned rolled oats

1 tablespoon brown sugar

1 teaspoon chia seeds

½ teaspoon ground cinnamon

1 cup oat milk

DIRECTIONS

1. Peel and chop the banana into small pieces.

2. Place them in a glass jar with walnuts, oats, brown sugar, chia seeds, and cinnamon. Stir to combine.

3. Pour in the milk and stir, making sure the oats are completely submerged in the milk.

4. Cover the jar and place it in the fridge.

5. Let it sit overnight.

6. Enjoy!

TIP

For a tropical twist, add a small amount of coconut flakes. The subtle infusion of coconut flavor will transport you to a breakfast paradise!

Sausage with Fried Eggs

Servings: 1 | **Prep + Cook Time:** 20 minutes

INGREDIENTS

2 breakfast sausage links

1 tablespoon butter

2 eggs

DIRECTIONS

1. Put a skillet over medium heat and let it preheat for 2-3 minutes.

2. Add the breakfast sausage links to the skillet.

3. Cook for about 3-5 minutes per side or until they are browned and cooked through.

4. Transfer the cooked sausages to a plate.

5. Crack the eggs in the same skillet and let the egg cook until the edges are crisp and golden and the yolk is cooked to your liking, about 2 minutes.

6. Transfer to the sausage plate. Enjoy!

TIP

For a touch of sweetness, you can glaze the sausages with maple syrup during the last minute of cooking.

FUN FACT

Sausage and eggs breakfast is its key role in the traditional English breakfast, also known as a "Full English." This hearty meal, a staple in British cuisine, combines sausage and eggs with other items like bacon, baked beans, and toast. Originally a luxury for the wealthy in Victorian England, it's now a beloved weekend treat worldwide, showcasing the enduring appeal of this classic combination.

Burrito Bowl

Servings: 1 | **Prep + Cook Time**: 10 minutes

INGREDIENTS

2 large eggs

Salt and black pepper to taste

1 large tortilla

¼ diced red bell pepper

¼ cup cooked bacon crumbles

1 tablespoon shredded Cheddar cheese

DIRECTIONS

1. Crack the eggs into a microwave-safe bowl. Whisk the eggs with a fork. Season with salt and pepper.

2. Transfer the bowl to the microwave. Microwave on high for 1 minute.

3. Using a clean spoon, "scramble" or break apart the eggs.

4. Warm the tortilla in the skillet over medium heat for a few seconds. Transfer it to a clean, flat surface. Cut into slices or triangles.

5. Arrange the ingredients in a small bowl or plate and enjoy.

TIP

To make your breakfast burrito even more flavorful, garnish with avocado slices, sour cream, or fresh herbs.

Homemade Hot Chocolate

Servings: 1 | **Prep + Cook Time:** 10 minutes

INGREDIENTS

1 cup whole milk

1 tablespoon of heavy cream

¼ teaspoon vanilla extract

1 tablespoon brown sugar

2 tablespoons unsweetened cocoa powder

DIRECTIONS

1. Pour the milk into a small saucepan over medium heat.

2. Add the heavy cream, vanilla extract, brown sugar, and cocoa powder.

3. Whisk frequently for a few minutes, until smooth.

4. Serve topped with marshmallows and grated chocolate, and enjoy.

TIP

For an extra touch of indulgence, add a pinch of sea salt to heighten the chocolate taste and a splash of vanilla extract for depth of flavor.

FUN FACT

A fun fact about hot chocolate is that it was originally a spicy and bitter drink made by the ancient Mayans, who mixed ground cocoa beans with water and chili peppers. It was only after Europeans added sugar and milk that it transformed into the sweet, creamy beverage we enjoy today.

SNACKS, SIDES & APPETIZERS

Air Fried French Fries

Servings: 1 | **Prep + Cook Time:** 35 minutes

INGREDIENTS

2 russet potatoes

1 tablespoon olive oil

Salt to taste

DIRECTIONS

1. Wash and peel the potatoes. Slice them lengthwise into ½-inch thick strips. Place the cut potatoes in a bowl of cold water and let them soak for 5 minutes. Drain the potatoes and pat them dry with paper towels.

2. In a bowl, whisk the olive oil and salt. Toss in the potatoes to coat.

3. Preheat the air fryer to 400°F for about 3 minutes.

4. Arrange them in a single and Air Fry for 18-20 minutes, shaking the basket or flipping the fries halfway through to ensure even cooking. Serve warm.

NOTE

Cooking times may vary depending on the size and type of your air fryer, so it's a good idea to check the fries periodically.

TIP

For oven-baked fries, preheat your oven to 420°F. Arrange the seasoned potatoes in a single layer on a baking sheet and bake them in the oven for 35 minutes, turning the fries halfway through the cooking time until they are golden brown and crispy.

Homemade Guacamole

Servings: 2 | **Prep Time:** 10 minutes

INGREDIENTS

1 avocado, peeled, pitted

¼ yellow onion, minced

1 lime wedge

1 small tomato

1 tablespoon fresh cilantro, chopped

Salt to taste

DIRECTIONS

1. Prepare all your ingredients and find a mixing bowl.

2. Cut the avocado in half.

3. Remove the pit, and scoop the flesh into a bowl.

4. Mash the avocado with a fork to your desired consistency.

5. Finely dice the onion and add it to the mashed avocado.

6. Squeeze the juice of the lime wedge into the bowl. Peel and chop the tomato and add it to the mixture.

7. Chop the fresh cilantro and add it to the bowl. Season with salt to taste. Gently mix all the ingredients together until well combined.

8. Taste the guacamole and adjust the lime juice, salt, or other ingredients according to your preference.

9. Transfer the guacamole to a serving bowl.

TIP

Serve the guacamole with tortilla chips, tacos, or as a topping for various dishes.

Crispy Fried Onion Rings

Servings: 2 | **Prep + Cook Time:** 30 minutes + soaking time

INGREDIENTS

1 onion

1 cup buttermilk

1 cup flour

1 teaspoon paprika

1/2 teaspoon salt

Vegetable oil for frying

DIRECTIONS

1. Peel the onion and slice it into 1/2-inch rings. Separate the rings and place them in a bowl.

2. Pour the buttermilk over them. Let them soak for at least 30 minutes. This helps tenderize the onions and adds flavor.

3. In a separate bowl, mix the flour, paprika, and salt.

4. Warm enough vegetable oil in a deep skillet to submerge the onion rings.

5. Coat the onion rings with the seasoned flour mixture. Shake off any excess flour.

6. Carefully place the coated onion rings into the hot oil. Fry them in batches for 2-3 minutes or until golden brown. Flip them halfway through for even cooking.

7. Remove the fried onion rings from the oil with a slotted spoon to a paper towel-lined plate to drain any excess oil. Serve and enjoy!

TIP

For an extra crunchy texture, double dip the onion rings in both the milk and the flour or breadcrumb mixture before frying.

Mozzarella Sticks

Servings: 2 | **Prep + Cook Time:** 40 minutes

INGREDIENTS

1/2 cup flour

1 egg

1 tablespoon milk

1 cup bread crumbs

¼ teaspoon salt

8 mozzarella sticks

2 teaspoons olive oil

½ cup marinara sauce

DIRECTIONS

1. Place the flour in a bowl. In another bowl, beat the egg and milk. In a third bowl, combine the crumbs and salt.

2. Roll the mozzarella sticks in flour, dredge in the egg mixture, and roll them in breadcrumbs. Shake off the excess between each step.

3. Arrange the coated mozzarella sticks on a tray lined with parchment paper and freeze them for about 15-20 minutes.

4. Preheat your oven to 400°F.

5. Transfer the frozen mozzarella sticks to a baking sheet. Bake them in the oven for 10-12 minutes or until golden and crispy.

6. Remove the mozzarella sticks from the oven. Let them cool for 2-3 minutes.

7. Serve with marinara sauce for dipping.

FUN FACT

By experimenting with different herbs in the breading or offering a range of dipping sauces from classic marinara to exotic chutneys, you can subtly introduce new tastes in a familiar format. This makes mozzarella sticks are a playful way to expand culinary horizons, especially for those who are usually hesitant to try new foods.

Vegetable Stir-Fry

Servings: 1 | **Prep + Cook Time:** 20 minutes

INGREDIENTS

½ zucchini

¼ onion

¼ green bell pepper

1 baby carrot

1 teaspoon olive oil

1 teaspoon soy sauce

1 cup cooked rice (optional)

DIRECTIONS

1. Cut the zucchini into half-moons. Slice the onion. Chop the green bell pepper. Thinly slice the baby carrot.

2. Warm the olive oil in a pan over medium-high heat. Add the vegetables. Stir-fry for about 10 minutes or until the vegetables are tender-crisp.

3. Drizzle the soy sauce over the vegetables and toss them to coat evenly.

4. Add the cooked rice (if you like) to the pan and stir until the rice is well combined with the vegetables.

5. Transfer the stir-fry to a plate. Enjoy!

FUN FACT

Making a vegetable stir-fry can be like creating your own colorful masterpiece? It's a fun way to "paint" with different vegetables, each adding its unique color and texture to the dish. Bright red peppers, green broccoli, purple eggplant, and orange carrots turn the stir-fry into a rainbow of colors. This not only makes the cooking process enjoyable and creative but also encourages to eat a variety of vegetables.

Air Fried Fish Fingers

Servings: 1 | **Prep + Cook Time:** 20 minutes

INGREDIENTS

Cooking spray

1 cod fillet, cut into sticks

½ cup flour

1 egg

¼ cup cornmeal

Salt to taste

¼ teaspoon paprika

1 lemon wedge

DIRECTIONS

1. Preheat your air fryer to 400°F for about 3 minutes.

2. Prepare three bowls. Place flour in one beat the egg in another, and put cornmeal mixed with a pinch of salt and paprika in the third.

3. Roll the sticks in the flour and shake off excess flour. Then, dip them in the egg. Lastly, dredge them in the cornmeal mixture.

4. Lightly spray the coated cod sticks with cooking spray.

5. Place fish fingers in the frying basket in a single layer, ensuring they are not overcrowded.

6. Select the Air Fry function and cook for 10-12 minutes, flipping the sticks halfway through until golden brown and crispy.

7. Squeeze the lemon wedge over the sticks before serving. Enjoy!

TIP

To make the fingers in a skillet, warm 2 tablespoons of vegetable oil over medium-high heat. Add the coated cod sticks and cook on each side for 3-4 minutes until golden brown and crispy.

Crunchy Baked Chicken Strips

Servings: 2 | **Prep + Cook Time**: 30 minutes

INGREDIENTS

Cooking spray

1 chicken breast, sliced into strips

½ cup breadcrumbs

½ tablespoon grated Parmesan cheese

½ teaspoon chicken seasoning

1 egg

½ cup ketchup

¼ teaspoon salt

DIRECTIONS

1. Preheat your oven to 400°F. Coat a baking sheet with cooking spray and set aside.

2. Cut the chicken breast into strips. Set aside.

3. Place the breadcrumbs, Parmesan cheese, chicken seasoning, and salt in a mixing bowl. Beat the egg in another mixing bowl.

4. Coat the chicken strips with the crumb mixture, then dip in the beaten eggs.

5. Arrange the coated chicken pieces on the greased baking sheet and bake for 15-20 minutes. Turn over halfway through cooking and cook for another 15 minutes until golden and crispy.

6. Serve immediately with ketchup.

7. Grab a bite, dip it in ketchup, and savor the deliciousness!

Sweet Potato Wedges

Servings: 2 | **Prep + Cook Time:** 50 minutes

INGREDIENTS

2 small sweet potatoes

1 tablespoon olive oil

1/2 teaspoon cornflour

1/4 teaspoon sweet paprika

Salt to taste

DIRECTIONS

1. Scrub the sweet potatoes if needed. Slice them in half on the long side, then cut each half again into two, the long side. You should obtain at least 8 long wedges.

2. Place the wedges in a bowl of cold water and let them soak for 10 minutes. Drain and pat them dry with kitchen paper.

3. Preheat your oven to 400°F and line a baking sheet with parchment paper.

4. Pour olive oil, cornflour, and sweet paprika into a bowl and stir well. Add the wedges and toss to coat.

5. Arrange the wedges on the baking sheet and bake in the oven for 40 minutes or until soft through the center and crispy on the outside, flipping them halfway through.

6. Remove from the oven and sprinkle with salt. Enjoy!

TIP

To prepare the potato wedges in Air Fryer, simply preheat your Air Fryer to 400°F for 3 minutes. Place the potatoes in the frying basket and AirFry them for 20-25 minutes, shaking once.

Corn Chowder

Servings: 2 | **Prep + Cook Time:** 30 minutes

INGREDIENTS

1 teaspoon olive oil

1 small onion

1 garlic clove

1 bell pepper

1 potato

2 cups chicken broth

1 cup frozen corn kernels

½ cup heavy cream

½ teaspoon ground cumin

Salt and pepper to taste

DIRECTIONS

1. Peel and finely chop the onion and garlic. Peel and mince the garlic clove. Wash the bell pepper, cut it in half, remove the seeds, and finely dice it. Peel the potato and chop it into cubes.

2. Warm the olive oil in a pot over medium heat. Add the chopped onion and garlic and sauté for 3 minutes or until soft.

3. Stir in the diced bell pepper and potato cubes for 1-2 minutes. Pour in the broth and bring the mixture to a boil.

4. Lower the heat and simmer for 15-20 minutes until the potatoes are tender. Add the corn and cook for 5 minutes.

5. Remove half of the soup from the pot and transfer it to a food processor. Blend until a creamy texture is achieved.

6. Return the blended soup to the pot. Stir in the heavy cream, cumin, salt, and pepper. Simmer for an additional 5 minutes.

7. Ladle the chowder into bowls and serve.

Fried Rice

Servings: 2 | **Prep + Cook Time:** 40 minutes

INGREDIENTS

1/2 cup white long-grain rice

1 tablespoon butter

1 egg

1/2 onion

1/2 carrot

1/4 cup frozen peas

1 garlic clove

1 teaspoon light soy sauce

1/4 teaspoon dried parsley

Salt and black pepper to taste

DIRECTIONS

1. Rinse the rice in a colander under cold running water until it runs clear, about 1 minute. Pour 1 cup of water into a small pot over medium heat and add a pinch of salt. Bring to a boil.

2. Pour in the rinsed rice and stir. Cover the pot with a lid and lower the heat. Simmer for 15 minutes.

3. While the rice is cooking, chop the onion and carrot, and peel and mince the garlic clove.

4. Whisk the egg in a small bowl.

5. Remove the rice from the heat and let it rest for a few minutes. Open the lid and set aside.

6. Melt the butter in a skillet over medium heat. Add onions, garlic, and carrots and sauté for 4-5 minutes. Stir in the peas. Push the ingredients to one side of the skillet and add the whisked egg. Scramble it and then mix it with the rest of the ingredients.

7. Sprinkle with salt, pepper, parsley, and drizzle with soy sauce. Cook for an additional 1-2 minutes, stirring often. Once done, remove it from the heat. Serve and enjoy!

Mashed Potatoes

Servings: 2 | **Prep + Cook Time:** 30 minutes

INGREDIENTS

4 potatoes

2 tablespoons butter

1/4 cup milk

Salt and black pepper to taste

DIRECTIONS

1. Peel the potatoes and cut them into chunks. Place the potato chunks in a pot, cover with cold water, and add a pinch of salt.

2. Bring to a boil, then reduce heat to simmer for 15-20 minutes or until the potatoes are fork-tender. Drain the potatoes through a colander and return them to the pot.

3. Mash the potatoes using a potato masher. Add the butter and mix until it melts.

4. Gradually pour the milk while mashing until the potatoes are creamy and smooth.

5. Season the mashed potatoes with salt and black pepper to taste. Enjoy!

TIP

To elevate your mashed potatoes to a whole new level, cook them with garlic cloves and a sprig of rosemary in the boiling water. This infuses the potatoes with aromatic flavors.

After draining them, adding the warmed milk and butter for creaminess, and mashing them to your desired consistency, finish by seasoning with salt, pepper, and a pinch of nutmeg for an extra depth of flavor. T

his combination creates a rich, flavorful, and unforgettable side dish.

Cornbread

Servings: 8 | **Prep + Cook Time:** 30 minutes

INGREDIENTS

1 cup all-purpose flour

1 cup fine cornmeal

1 teaspoon baking powder

1/2 teaspoon baking soda

1/8 teaspoon salt

1/2 cup butter, melted, slightly cooled

1/3 cup packed light brown sugar

1 1/2 tablespoons honey

1 large egg, at room temperature

1 cup buttermilk, at room temperature

DIRECTIONS

1. Preheat your oven to 400° F. Grease, lightly flour a 9-inch square baking pan, then set it aside.

2. Whisk together the cornmeal, flour, baking powder, baking soda, and salt in a large bowl. Set this aside.

3. Mix the melted butter, brown sugar, and honey thoroughly in a medium bowl until smooth and thick. Whisk in the egg until thoroughly combined. Then, incorporate the buttermilk.

4. Gently pour the wet ingredients into the dry ingredients and stir until just combined, being careful not to over-mix.

5. Pour the batter into the prepared baking pan. Bake for about 20 minutes until the top is golden brown and a toothpick inserted into the center comes clean. The edges should be slightly crispy.

6. Allow the cornbread to cool a bit before slicing and serving. Enjoy it with butter, honey, jam, or your favorite cornbread accompaniments.

Simple Risotto

Servings: 2 | **Prep + Cook Time:** 35 minutes

INGREDIENTS

½ onion

1 garlic clove

1 tablespoon olive oil

1 tablespoon grated Parmesan cheese

2 ¼ cups chicken stock

1 cup Arborio rice

1 tablespoon butter

Salt and black pepper to taste

DIRECTIONS

1. Peel and finely chop the onion and garlic.

2. Heat the chicken broth in a small pot and keep it warm on low heat

3. In a saucepan, warm the olive oil over medium heat. Add the chopped onion to the hot oil and sauté for 3 minutes. Add the rice. Toast the rice for about 2 minutes until it becomes slightly translucent at the edges.

4. Gradually pour the warm broth one ladle at a time, stirring frequently. Allow the liquid to be mostly absorbed before adding the next ladle. Continue this process until the rice is creamy and cooked to al dente texture, about 18-20 minutes.

5. Remove the saucepan from the heat, stir in the butter and Parmesan cheese until melted, and season with salt and pepper to taste. Enjoy!

FUN FACT

When you start, risotto rice looks ordinary and simple. But as you stir and add broth, it slowly transforms into a creamy, delicious dish. This change happens because the special type of rice used in risotto, like Arborio or Carnaroli, releases starch as it cooks, which creates its signature creamy texture! Mastering risotto is about understanding the subtle balance of flavors and textures, which is why in many culinary circles, a perfectly cooked risotto is a sign of a truly skilled cook

Creamy Corn

Servings: 6 | **Prep + Cook Time:** 15 minutes

INGREDIENTS

2 tablespoons unsalted butter

5 cups fresh corn kernels

1/2 cup heavy cream

3/4 teaspoon salt

1/2 teaspoon black pepper

1 1/2 tablespoons granulated sugar

Pinch of cayenne pepper

Pinch of ground nutmeg

1 cup whole milk

3 tablespoons flour

DIRECTIONS

1. In a medium saucepan, melt the butter over medium heat.

2. Add the fresh corn kernels, heavy cream salt, pepper, sugar, cayenne pepper, and nutmeg to the saucepan. Stir everything together to ensure it's well combined.

3. In a separate small bowl or a large measuring cup, whisk the milk and flour together until smooth. Then, pour this mixture into the saucepan with the corn.

4. Cook the mixture, stirring constantly, for about 5 minutes or until it thickens.

5. Taste and adjust the seasoning with additional salt, pepper, sugar, cayenne pepper, and nutmeg as needed.

FUN FACT

Did you know that creamy corn gets its unique texture not just from cream but also from the natural properties of corn itself? When corn is cooked and stirred, it releases a milky substance known as "corn milk." This corn milk, combined with the natural starches in the corn, helps to thicken the dish and give it its creamy consistency. This means that the creaminess of the dish can be enhanced even without adding a lot of extra cream or dairy products, making it a naturally luscious and comforting food. It's a wonderful example of how simple cooking techniques can bring out the best in fresh, everyday ingredients!

Corn on the Cob

Servings: 2 | **Prep + Cook Time:** 30 minutes

INGREDIENTS

2 ears of corn

1 tablespoon butter

Salt to taste

DIRECTIONS

1. Husk the corn, removing both the husk and silk.

2. Bring a large pot of water to a boil over medium heat.

3. Add the corn and boil for about 5-7 minutes or until the kernels are tender.

4. Remove the corn from the pot to a plate.

5. Spread butter evenly over the kernels. The heat will help melt the butter.

6. Sprinkle with salt. Enjoy!

FUN FACT

Did you know that each strand of silk on a corn cob is connected to an individual kernel? This silk is essential for the corn's growth, as it catches pollen needed for each kernel to develop. So, when you're husking corn on the cob, you're actually seeing a crucial part of how corn grows!

SALADS, SOUPS, & STEWS

Tropical Fruit Salad

Servings: 1 | **Prep Time:** 15 minutes

INGREDIENTS

1 fresh pineapple round

4 strawberries

1/2 mango

1/2 banana

1 teaspoon honey

1 teaspoon shredded coconut

2 fresh mint leaves

DIRECTIONS

1. Cut fresh pineapple into bite-sized chunks. Hull and quarter the strawberries. Dice the mango into delightful pieces.

2. Slice the banana. Place the fruit in a salad bowl and mix. Drizzle with honey and sprinkle with coconut.

3. Refrigerate the fruit salad for about 10 minutes. Garnish with fresh mint leaves and enjoy!

FUN FACT

Did you know that fruit salad can actually change flavor over time, even in the fridge? This happens because as the fruits sit together, they start to share their juices and flavors with each other. This natural process turns every bowl of fruit salad into a constantly evolving flavor experience

Waldorf Salad

Servings: 1 | **Prep Time:** 15 minutes

INGREDIENTS

1/2 red apple

1/2 green apple

1/2 cup celery

3 walnuts

1/4 cup seedless grapes

2 tablespoons mayonnaise

1 tablespoon lemon juice

1 tablespoon honey

A pinch of salt

DIRECTIONS

1. Peel and dice the red and green apples into bite-sized pieces.

2. Thinly slice the celery. Chop the walnuts. Halve the grapes.

3. Transfer the diced apples, sliced celery, chopped walnuts, and halved grapes to a bowl.

4. Mix the mayonnaise, lemon juice, honey, and salt in a small bowl.

5. Pour the resulting dressing over the fruit and nut mixture.

6. Gently toss everything to coat.

FUN FACT

Did you know that the Waldorf Salad is known for its celebrity endorsement? It gained fame when it became a favorite of former First Lady of the United States, Helen Taft, in the early 1900s. Her love for the salad popularized it even more, and it eventually became a staple in American cuisine. Today, the Waldorf Salad has stood the test of time and is enjoyed by everyone, making it a true culinary icon with a presidential seal of approval!

Caprese Salad

Servings: 1 | **Prep Time:** 10 minutes

INGREDIENTS

1 tomato

½ fresh mozzarella cheese ball

3 fresh basil leaves

1 tablespoon extra-virgin olive oil

½ tablespoon balsamic vinegar

Salt to taste

DIRECTIONS

1. Wash the tomato and slice it into rounds.

2. Slice the fresh mozzarella into rounds similar in thickness to the tomato slices.

3. Arrange the tomato and mozzarella slices on a plate, slightly overlapping.

4. Season with salt and drizzle with balsamic vinegar and extra-virgin olive oil.

5. Garnish with basil leaves.

FUN FACT

Did you know that the Caprese Salad is often associated with the colors of the Italian flag? This classic Italian dish features red tomatoes, white mozzarella cheese, and green basil leaves, mirroring the tricolor flag of Italy. It's not just a delicious salad but also a patriotic representation of Italian cuisine!

Grilled Chicken Salad

Servings: 1 | **Prep + Cook Time:** 30 minutes

INGREDIENTS

1 boneless, skinless chicken breast half

1 cup baby spinach

½ cup arugula

2 Romain lettuce leaves

4 cherry tomatoes

1/4 cucumber

3 green olives

1 tablespoon grated Parmesan cheese

1 tablespoon olive oil

1 tablespoon apple cider vinegar

Salt and black pepper to taste

DIRECTIONS

1. Preheat a grill pan over medium-high heat. Season the chicken breast with salt and pepper.

2. Add the chicken to the pan and grill it for 5-6 minutes per side. Allow the grilled chicken to rest for a few minutes, then slice it into thin strips.

3. Torn the lettuce leaves into bite-size pieces. Halve the cherry tomatoes and slice the cucumber. Place the baby spinach, arugula, lettuce, cherry tomatoes, cucumber slices, and olives in a bowl.

4. Top with the sliced grilled chicken. Drizzle with apple cider vinegar and olive oil. Gently toss the salad to combine all the ingredients and coat them in the dressing.

5. Sprinkle Parmesan cheese and serve.

TIP

If you want an Asian twist to this classic salad, substitute the chicken for grilled tofu or tempeh.They are excellent sources of protein for a vegetarian or vegan salad. Other alternatives include grilled portobello mushrooms or chickpeas.

Tomato & Cucumber Salad

Servings: 1 | **Prep Time:** 10 minutes

INGREDIENTS

1 medium tomato

1/2 cucumber, diced

1 green onion

1 small feta cheese slice

1 tablespoon fresh parsley leaves

1 tablespoon extra-virgin olive oil

1 tablespoon balsamic vinegar

Salt to taste

DIRECTIONS

1. Cut the tomato and cucumber into rounds. Finely chop the green onion and parsley leaves.

2. Transfer the sliced tomato, cucumber rounds, chopped green onion, and parsley leaves to a bowl.

3. Generously crumble feta cheese over the vegetables.

4. Combine extra-virgin olive oil, balsamic vinegar, and a pinch of salt in a small jar. Cover with a lid and shake well to create the dressing.

5. Pour the prepared dressing over the vegetables. Gently toss everything to coat.

6. Transfer the salad to a plate and enjoy!

FUN FACT

Commonly known as "Greek Salad" in many parts of the world, despite its roots not being exclusively Greek. While it does share similarities with traditional Greek cuisine, the salad has countless variations across Mediterranean cuisine.

Cobb Salad

Servings: 1 | **Prep Time:** 15 minutes

INGREDIENTS

1/2 teaspoon red wine vinegar

1/2 teaspoon yellow mustard

1 tablespoon olive oil

Salt and pepper to taste

1 cup mixed salad greens

1/2 cup cooked chicken breast

1 hard-boiled egg

4 cherry tomatoes

1/4 cup cucumber

2 tablespoons crumbled blue cheese

2 crispy bacon slices

DIRECTIONS

1. Dice the cooked chicken breast. Peel and quarter the hard-boiled egg and halve the cherry tomatoes.

2. Slice the cucumber into rounds and crumble the bacon slices.

3. In a jar, shake together red wine vinegar, yellow mustard, olive oil, salt, and black pepper to create the dressing.

4. Spread mixed greens on a salad plate.

5. Arrange rows of chicken, quartered hard-boiled egg, halved cherry tomatoes, cucumber rounds, crumbled blue cheese, and bacon.

6. Drizzle the salad with the prepared dressing and enjoy!

Simple Coleslaw

Servings: 1 | **Prep Time:** 10 minutes

INGREDIENTS

1/2 teaspoon honey

1 tablespoon mayonnaise

1/2 teaspoon Dijon mustard

1/2 teaspoon apple cider vinegar

1/2 cup shredded green cabbage

1/2 cup shredded red cabbage

1/4 cup shredded carrots

Salt and black pepper to taste

DIRECTIONS

1. Mix honey, mayonnaise, Dijon mustard, and apple cider vinegar in a small bowl until well combined.

2. In a separate bowl, combine the shredded cabbage and carrots.

3. Pour the dressing over the vegetables and toss until the cabbage and carrots are evenly coated.

4. Season with salt and pepper.

5. Transfer the coleslaw to a serving bowl and enjoy!

FUN FACT

Did you know that coleslaw has been enjoyed for centuries? It dates back to ancient times when the Romans and Greeks made a similar dish using cabbage and various dressings. In the 18th century, Dutch immigrants introduced coleslaw to America, and it has since become a staple in American cuisine, especially at summer barbecues and picnics. So, when you're savoring a bowl of coleslaw, you're enjoying a dish with a rich history that spans cultures and centuries!

Potato & Bacon Salad with Mustard Dressing

Servings: 1 | **Prep Time:** 25 minutes

INGREDIENTS

1 potato

2 bacon slices

1 green onion

1 tablespoon apple cider vinegar

1/2 tablespoon yellow mustard

1/2 tablespoon olive oil

Salt and black pepper to taste

1/2 tablespoon fresh parsley leaves

DIRECTIONS

1. Peel and dice the potato into bite-sized cubes. Transfer them to a water-filled small pot over medium heat. Boil until tender. Drain and let them cool slightly.

2. Heat a pan over medium heat. Add the bacon and cook for 3 minutes or until crispy. Remove it from the pan and let it cool. Once cooled, crumble it.

3. In a small jar, whisk together apple cider vinegar, Dijon mustard, olive oil, salt, and black pepper.

4. Add the finely chopped onion to the same pan used for bacon. Sauté it for 3 minutes or until it becomes translucent.

5. Combine the boiled and diced potato, crumbled bacon, and sautéed onions In a mixing bowl. Pour the prepared dressing over the potato mixture. Gently toss to coat.

6. Garnish with chopped fresh parsley. Enjoy!

Black-Eyed Peas Salad

Servings: 1 | **Prep Time:** 10 minutes

INGREDIENTS

1/4 cup cherry tomatoes

1/4 cup cucumber, diced

1/4 red onion, finely chopped

1 tablespoon fresh cilantro leaves

1 tablespoon crumbled feta cheese

1/2 cup canned black-eyed peas, drained

1 tablespoon olive oil

1 tablespoon balsamic vinegar

Salt and black pepper to taste

DIRECTIONS

1. Halve the cherry tomatoes.

2. Chop the cucumber, red onion, and cilantro leaves.

3. Drain and rinse the canned black-eyed peas.

4. In a small bowl, whisk together olive oil, balsamic vinegar, salt, and pepper to create the dressing.

5. Place the black-eyed peas, cherry tomatoes, cucumber, red onion, cilantro, and feta cheese in a bowl.

6. Toss the ingredients to combine.

7. Pour the prepared dressing over the vegetables.

8. Toss the salad until everything is well coated.

9. Transfer the salad to a plate. Bon appétit!

TIP

If you like to substitute the black-eyed peas, you can do it for canned black beans or chickpeas. They have similarly rich texture and taste and are an excellent choice too.

Vegetable Soup

Servings: 2 | **Prep + Cook Time:** 30 minutes

INGREDIENTS

1 potato

1 baby carrot

1/4 cup green peas

1/4 celery stalk

1/2 small onion

1 garlic clove

1 small tomato

2 cups vegetable broth

1/4 teaspoon dried thyme

Salt and black pepper to taste

1 teaspoon olive oil

1 teaspoon fresh parsley leaves

DIRECTIONS

1. Peel the potato, rinse it under cold water, and cut it into bite-sized cubes.

2. Clean the baby carrot and thinly slice it.

3. Chop the celery, onion, and parsley leaves. Mince the garlic clove and dice the tomato.

4. Warm olive oil in a small pot over medium heat. Add chopped onions and minced garlic. Sauté until onions are translucent.

5. Add the prepared vegetables to the pot.

6. Stir and cook for 3-4 minutes until slightly tender.

7. Pour in the vegetable broth and add the diced tomatoes. Stir well. Add dried thyme, salt, and pepper to the soup.

8. Bring the soup to a gentle boil, then reduce the heat to low. Cover and simmer for about 15 minutes or until the vegetables are cooked.

9. Garnish the vegetable soup with fresh parsley and enjoy!

Chicken Noodle Soup

Servings: 2 | **Prep + Cook Time:** 30 minutes

INGREDIENTS

2 skinless and boneless chicken thighs

1/4 cup egg noodles

1/2 carrot

1/2 parsnip

1/4 celery stalk

1 shallot

1 garlic clove

2 cups chicken broth

Salt and black pepper to taste

1 teaspoon olive oil

1 tablespoon fresh parsley leaves

DIRECTIONS

1. Chop the shallot and mince the garlic clove. Thinly slice the carrot and parsnip. Finely chop the celery. Chop the fresh parsley leaves.

2. Dice the chicken thighs into bite-sized pieces. Season with salt and pepper.

3. Warm olive oil in a pot over medium heat.

4. Add the diced chicken pieces and brown them on both sides. Set aside.

5. Add the chopped shallot, minced garlic clove, sliced carrots, and parsnip to the same pot and sauté them until fragrant, about 5 minutes.

6. Return the browned chicken to the pot.

7. Pour in chicken broth. Cover and simmer for 15-20 minutes or until chicken is cooked.

8. Add the egg noodles to the pot and cook according to package instructions.

9. Season soup with salt and black pepper.

10. Sprinkle the chopped parsley over the soup. Enjoy!

Beef & Bean Stew

Servings: 2 | **Prep + Cook Time:** 30 minutes

INGREDIENTS

1/2 pound ground beef

1/2 onion

1 garlic clove

1/2 bell pepper

1/4 cup canned kidney beans

1/4 cup canned diced tomatoes

1 cup beef broth

1/4 teaspoon cumin

Salt and black pepper to taste

1 teaspoon vegetable oil

1 tablespoon fresh parsley leaves

DIRECTIONS

1. Peel and finely chop the onion and garlic clove.

2. Chop the bell pepper. Drain and rinse the kidney beans.

3. Chop the fresh parsley leaves.

4. Warm the vegetable oil in a small pot over medium heat.

5. Add the chopped onions, garlic, and bell peppers. Sauté for 4 minutes or until softened.

6. Add ground beef to the pot.

7. Break it up with a spoon and cook until browned, about 6 minutes.

8. Sprinkle cumin, salt, and pepper over the beef.

9. Stir well to coat the meat with the seasonings. Stir in kidney beans and diced tomatoes (with their juice).

10. Pour in beef broth and stir. Bring the mixture to a simmer.

11. Reduce heat to low, cover the pot, and let the stew simmer for about 15 minutes.

12. Garnish with chopped parsley. Enjoy!

COOKING FOR YOU

Roast Beef Sandwich

Servings: 1 | **Prep + Cook Time:** 10 minutes

INGREDIENTS

3 roast beef slices

2 whole grain bread slices

1 tablespoon mayonnaise

1 teaspoon Dijon mustard

1 lettuce leaves

3 tomato slices

Salt and pepper to taste

DIRECTIONS

1. On one slice of bread, spread mayonnaise, and on the other, spread Dijon mustard.

2. Place the roast beef slices on one of the bread slices.

3. Top the roast beef with lettuce leaves and tomato slices.

4. Sprinkle with salt and pepper.

5. Place the second slice of bread on top, condiment side down, to create a sandwich.

6. Cut the sandwich in half diagonally. Enjoy!

FUN FACT

In present-day America, the roast beef sandwich is like a culinary road trip, with each region adding its twist. From New York's classic kaiser roll to Los Angeles' famous French dip, it's a delicious showcase of regional creativity.

Cheeseburger

Servings: 1 | **Prep + Cook Time:** 15 minutes

INGREDIENTS

1/4 pound ground beef

Salt and black pepper to taste

1 hamburger bun

1 Cheddar cheese slice

1 lettuce leaf

1 tomato slice

1/4 teaspoon ketchup

1/4 teaspoon mustard

1/4 teaspoon mayonnaise

DIRECTIONS

1. Season the ground beef with salt and pepper.

2. Gently shape it into a patty.

3. Preheat your grill over medium-high heat.

4. Place the beef patty on the hot grill and cook for approximately 4 minutes per side or until it reaches your desired level of doneness.

5. In the last minute of cooking, place the Cheddar cheese slice on top of the patty to melt.

6. Cut the hamburger bun in half. Toast the bun on the grill.

7. Place the cooked patty with melted cheese on the bottom half of the bun.

8. Add lettuce, tomato, ketchup, mustard, and mayonnaise.

9. Place the top half of the bun over the toppings to complete your burger.

10. Serve and enjoy!

Spaghetti Bolognese

Servings: 2 | **Prep Time:** 20 minutes

INGREDIENTS

1/2 pound spaghetti

1 tablespoon olive oil

1/2 onion

1 clove garlic

1/4 carrots

1/4 celery stalk

1/4 pound ground beef

1/2 cup canned crushed tomatoes

1 tablespoon tomato paste

1/4 teaspoon dried oregano

1/4 teaspoon dried basil

Salt and black pepper to taste

1 tablespoon grated Parmesan cheese

DIRECTIONS

1. Bring a large pot of salted water over medium heat to a boil. Break the spaghetti in half. Add the spaghetti to the pot.

2. Cook according to the package instructions. Drain and set aside.

3. Dice the onion, garlic, carrots, and celery. Warm the olive oil in a pan over medium heat. Add the diced onion, garlic, carrots, and celery and sauté for 5 minutes or until softened.

4. Stir in the ground beef to the pan. Cook until browned, breaking it apart with a spoon as it cooks.

5. Add the tomato paste, crushed tomatoes, dried oregano, dried basil, salt, and pepper. Stir well to combine.

6. Reduce the heat to low and let the sauce simmer for 10-15 minutes.

7. Add the cooked spaghetti to the pan and toss until the pasta is coated evenly with the sauce.

8. Transfer the spaghetti Bolognese to a plate. Sprinkle with grated Parmesan cheese, and enjoy!

Quesadillas

Servings: 1 | Prep + Cooking time: 15 minutes

INGREDIENTS

Toppings: sour cream, guacamole, salsa (optional)

1/2 cup of shredded Monterey Jack cheese

1/3 cup of shredded Pepper Jack cheese

Nonstick cooking spray

1/3 cup of cream cheese

2 flour tortillas

1/2 cup of shredded cheddar cheese

1 small diced tomato

DIRECTIONS

1. Coat a medium-sized frying pan with nonstick spray and heat it over a medium-high setting, for about a minute. Spread the cream cheese uniformly on one side of each tortilla using a butter knife.

2. Place one tortilla in the pan, cream cheese side up, and evenly sprinkle with all the cheese and diced tomato. Cover with the second tortilla, placing it cream cheese side down.

3. Cook for 3 minutes or until the cheese starts to melt. Check if the bottom tortilla has turned golden brown by slightly lifting an edge. If so, flip the quesadilla over with a spatula and cook for 2 minutes until the other side turns golden brown.

4. Once done, transfer the quesadilla to a cutting board, slice it into triangle pieces, and serve with your choice of toppings.

TIP

For a bean and cheese quesadilla, spread 2 tablespoons of refried beans evenly over the cream cheese, then sprinkle with shredded cheese.

For a chicken and cheese quesadilla, add 1/4 cup cubed or shredded cooked chicken to the cheese before covering it with the second tortilla.

Chicken Skewers

Servings: 1 | **Prep + Cook Time:** 25 minutes

INGREDIENTS

Wooden skewers, soaked in water for 30 minutes

1 boneless, skinless chicken breast, cut

1 tablespoon olive oil

1 clove garlic, minced

1/2 teaspoon dried oregano

1/2 teaspoon smoked paprika

Salt and pepper to taste

DIRECTIONS

1. Cut the chicken breast into bite-sized cubes.

2. Peel and mince the garlic clove.

3. Place the olive oil, minced garlic, dried oregano, smoked paprika, salt, and pepper in a bowl and stir to combine.

4. Add the chicken cubes and toss to coat. Let it marinate for at least 10 minutes.

5. Thread the marinated chicken onto 2 skewers, distributing evenly.

6. Preheat a grill pan over medium-high heat.

7. Grill the skewers for 4-5 minutes on each side or until the chicken is cooked through and has a nice char.

8. Remove the skewers from the pan and let them rest for a minute. Enjoy!

TIP

Serve the grilled chicken skewers with your favorite dipping sauce or over a bed of rice.

Veggie Burger

Servings: 2 | **Prep + Cook Time**: 15 minutes

INGREDIENTS

1 tablespoon olive oil

1 veggie burger patty (store-bought)

1 whole-grain burger bun

1 tablespoon mayonnaise

1 teaspoon Dijon mustard

2 lettuce leaves

2 tomato slices

3 red onion slices

2 pickles

Salt and black pepper to taste

DIRECTIONS

1. Warm the olive oil in a skillet over medium heat.

2. Cook the patty for 10-12 minutes, flipping half way.

3. Meanwhile, cut the burger bun in half and lightly toast in the skillet pan for a few minutes until golden.

4. In a small bowl, mix mayonnaise and Dijon mustard.

5. Spread this sauce on the cut sides of the burger bun.

6. Place lettuce leaves on the bottom half of the bun.

7. Top with the cooked veggie patty.

8. Layer tomato, red onion, and pickles on top of the veggie patty.

9. Sprinkle with salt and pepper.

10. Place the top half of the bun over the toppings, creating a complete burger.

11. Enjoy!

Chicken Alfredo Pasta

Servings: 1 | **Prep + Cook Time:** 15 minutes

INGREDIENTS

1/4 pound fettuccine pasta

1 tablespoon olive oil

1/2 tablespoon butter

1/4/2 chicken breast

1/4 cup heavy cream

2 tablespoons grated Parmesan cheese

Salt and black pepper to taste

3 fresh basil leaves

DIRECTIONS

1. Boil salted water in a pot over medium heat.

2. Stir in fettuccine and cook according to package directions. Drain and set aside.

3. Cut the chicken breast into bite-sized pieces.

4. Warm the olive oil in a saucepan over medium heat.

5. Add the chicken breast and cook until no longer pink, about 5 minutes.

6. Add butter to the saucepan and stir until melted.

7. Pour in the heavy cream and mix well. Simmer for 2-3 minutes until it slightly thickens.

8. Stir in the grated Parmesan cheese until melted.

9. Season the sauce with salt and black pepper.

10. Add the cooked fettuccine pasta to the Alfredo sauce.

11. Toss until the pasta is well-coated in the creamy sauce.

12. Garnish with fresh basil. Bon appétit!

Bean & Cheese Burrito

Servings: 1 | **Prep + Cook Time:** 10 minutes

INGREDIENTS

1 flour tortilla

1/2 cup canned black beans

1/4 cup shredded cheddar cheese

2 tablespoons salsa

2 tablespoons sour cream

1 green onion, finely chopped

Salt and pepper to taste

DIRECTIONS

1. Heat a dry skillet over medium heat. Warm the flour tortilla for about 10 seconds to make it pliable. Set aside.

2. Drain and rinse the black beans and transfer them to the skillet. Stir for 1 minute until warm. Season with salt and pepper.

3. Place the warmed tortilla on a flat surface. In the center of the tortilla, add the black beans. Sprinkle with shredded cheddar cheese.

4. Spoon salsa over the cheese. Fold the sides of the tortilla towards the center, then roll it up from the bottom to create a burrito.

5. Place the burrito seam-side down on a plate. Top it with dollops of sour cream and chopped green onions.

6. Enjoy!

FUN FACT

A fun fact about the burrito is that its name, "burrito," actually means "little donkey" in Spanish. The origin of this name is believed to be a reference to the way the ingredients are rolled up inside the tortilla, resembling the packs that donkeys used to carry. So, when you're enjoying a burrito, you're savoring a tasty "little donkey" of deliciousness!

Roasted Chicken Drumsticks

Servings: 1 | **Prep + Cook Time:** 40 minutes

INGREDIENTS

2 chicken drumsticks

1 tablespoon olive oil

1 teaspoon garlic powder

1 teaspoon paprika

1/4 teaspoon dried thyme

1/4 teaspoon dried rosemary

Salt and black pepper to taste

DIRECTIONS

1. Preheat your oven to 420°F.

2. Place the olive oil, garlic powder, paprika, dried thyme, rosemary, salt, and pepper in a small bowl and stir to combine.

3. Pat the chicken drumsticks dry with paper towels.

4. Add them to the prepared seasoning mixture and toss to coat.

5. Line a small baking sheet with parchment paper.

6. Place the seasoned drumsticks on the sheet.

7. Roast the drumsticks in the preheated oven for approximately 30 minutes or until the skin is golden and the meat is cooked with no traces of pink.

8. Turn them halfway through the cooking time for even browning.

9. Pierce the thickest part of a drumstick with a knife.

10. The chicken is done if the juices run clear and there's no pink near the bone.

11. Let the roasted chicken drumsticks rest for a few minutes before serving. Enjoy!

Breaded Fish Fillets

Servings: 1 | **Prep + Cook Time:** 20 minutes

INGREDIENTS

1/2 cup breadcrumbs

1 tablespoon grated Parmesan cheese

1/2 teaspoon fish seasoning

1/2 teaspoon lemon zest

Salt and black pepper to taste

1 egg

1 tilapia fillet

1 tablespoon olive oil

2 lemon wedges

DIRECTIONS

1. Preheat your oven to 410°F.

2. Place the breadcrumbs, grated Parmesan cheese, fish seasoning, salt, and black pepper in a shallow dish and stir to combine. In another dish, beat the egg.

3. Pat the tilapia fillet dry with paper towels. Dip the fish fillet into the beaten egg, then dredge it in the breadcrumb mixture, pressing gently to adhere the breadcrumbs.

4. Warm the olive oil in an oven-safe skillet over medium-high heat. Place the breaded fish fillet in the hot skillet and sear for 2-3 minutes on each side until golden brown.

5. Transfer the skillet to the preheated oven and bake for 5-7 minutes or until the fish is cooked and flakes easily with a fork.

6. Remove the fish from the oven and let it rest for a minute. Serve it with lemon wedges. Enjoy!

TIP

If you don't have tilapia, use other fish fillets such as cod, haddock, flounder, or pollock. They taste just as good.

Country Fried Steak

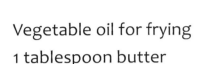

Servings: 1 | **Prep + Cook Time:** 30 minutes

INGREDIENTS

1 beef cube steak (about 4-6 ounces)

1/2 cup all-purpose flour

1/4 teaspoon paprika

Salt and pepper to taste

1/2 cup buttermilk

Vegetable oil for frying

1 tablespoon butter

1 tablespoon cornstarch

1 cup milk

DIRECTIONS

1. Mix the flour, paprika, salt, and pepper in a shallow bowl.

2. Pat the cube steak dry with paper towels.

3. Dredge the steak in the buttermilk, then dip it in the flour mixture, ensuring it's evenly coated.

4. Press the flour mixture onto the steak to help it adhere.

5. Warm about 1/4 inch of vegetable oil in a skillet over medium-high heat. Once the oil is hot, carefully place the breaded steak in the skillet to prevent splattering.

6. Fry for 3-4 minutes per side or until golden brown and cooked through. Transfer the fried steak to a plate lined with paper towels to drain any excess oil.

7. Add the butter to the skillet to melt. In a small bowl, mix the milk with cornstarch.

8. Pour this mixture into the skillet and stir constantly for about 3 minutes or until the gravy is thickened.

9. Season with salt and pepper. Return the steak to the skillet and flip it to coat with gravy. Cook for 1-2 minutes. Enjoy!

Chicken Wings

Servings: 1 | **Prep + Cook Time:** 30 minutes

INGREDIENTS

4-5 chicken wings

1/4 cup all-purpose flour

Salt and black pepper to taste

1/4 cup Carolina barbecue sauce

DIRECTIONS

1. Preheat your oven to 400°F. Line a baking sheet with parchment paper and set aside.

2. Pat the chicken wings dry with paper towels. Place the flour, salt, and pepper in a bowl and stir to combine.

3. Add the chicken wings to the flour mixture and toss them to coat

4. Arrange the coated wings on the prepared baking sheet and bake in the oven for about 20 minutes or until the wings are golden and crispy.

5. Remove the chicken wings from the oven and toss in Carolina barbecue sauce. Enjoy!

FUN FACT

It wasn't until the 1960s in Buffalo, New York, that chicken wings gained popularity as a snack food. A local bar, the Anchor Bar, is credited with creating the first Buffalo chicken wings by deep-frying them and tossing them in a spicy sauce. From there, they became a sensation, and now, chicken wings are a beloved staple at parties, sports events, and restaurants worldwide. Time to cook them at home!

Sloppy Joes

Servings: 1 | **Prep + Cook Time:** 25 minutes

INGREDIENTS

1/4 onion

1 clove garlic

1/4 cup red bell pepper

1/4 pound ground beef

1 teaspoon olive oil

2 tablespoons ketchup

1 tablespoon tomato paste

1/2 tablespoon brown sugar

1/2 tablespoon Worcestershire sauce

1/2 teaspoon mustard

Salt and black pepper to taste

1 hamburger bun

DIRECTIONS

1. Finely chop the onion, garlic clove, and bell pepper.

2. Warm the olive oil in a skillet over medium heat.

3. Add and cook the ground beef for 6 minutes or until browned. Break it into crumbles as it cooks.

4. Add chopped onion, bell pepper, and garlic to the skillet.

5. Cook for an additional 3-4 minutes until the vegetables are softened. Season the mixture with salt and pepper.

6. Place the ketchup, tomato paste, brown sugar, Worcestershire sauce, and mustard in a small bowl and mix well.

7. Pour the sauce into the skillet with the beef and vegetables. Stir to combine, and let it simmer for 5-7 minutes.

8. While the mixture simmers, toast the hamburger bun.

9. Spoon the sloppy joe mixture onto the bottom half of the toasted bun. Top with the other half.

10. Serve and enjoy!

Chicken Enchilada

Servings: 1 | **Prep + Cook Time:** 25 minutes

INGREDIENTS

1/2 cup shredded cooked chicken

1/4 cup black beans

1/4 cup frozen corn kernels

1 tomato

1/4 red bell peppers

2 tablespoons enchilada sauce

1/4 teaspoon ground cumin

Salt and black pepper to taste

1 flour tortilla

1/4 cup grated Mexican cheese blend

1 tablespoon fresh cilantro leaves

1 tablespoon sour cream

DIRECTIONS

1. Drain and rinse the black beans; set aside.

2. Dice the tomato and bell pepper.

3. Chop the fresh cilantro leaves; reserve.

4. Place the shredded chicken, black beans, corn, diced tomatoes, diced bell peppers, enchilada sauce, ground cumin, salt, and pepper in a bowl. Mix well.

5. Put the flour tortilla in a small oven-safe dish. Spoon the chicken mixture onto the tortilla. Sprinkle with shredded Mexican cheese.

6. Bake in the preheated oven for about 12-15 minutes or until the cheese is melted and bubbly and the edges of the tortilla are golden.

7. Remove from the oven and transfer to a plate.

8. Add a dollop of sour cream and garnish with chopped fresh cilantro. Enjoy!

Chicken Tenders

Servings: 1 | **Prep + Cook Time:** 25 minutes

INGREDIENTS

Cooking spray

4 chicken tenders

1/2 cup flour

1/4 teaspoon paprika

Salt and black pepper to taste

1/2 cup buttermilk

1/2 cup breadcrumbs

DIRECTIONS

1. Preheat your oven to 400°F.

2. Set up three shallow bowls. In the first bowl, add combine flour, paprika, salt, and pepper.

3. In the second bowl, place the buttermilk.

4. In the third bowl, add breadcrumbs.

5. Dip the chicken tenders into the flour mixture, coating evenly.

6. Shake off excess flour.

7. Next, dip the floured chicken into the buttermilk, ensuring it's well-coated.

8. Finally, dredge it in the breadcrumbs, pressing down to adhere the crumbs.

9. Lightly spray the chicken tenders with cooking spray.

10. Bake in the oven for 12-15 minutes or until golden brown and cooked through.

11. Remove from the oven and let them cool for a few minutes. Serve and enjoy!

Chipotle Chicken Wrap

Servings: 1 | Prep + Cooking time: 10 minutes

INGREDIENTS

1/3 cup chipotle mayo

1 cup cooked (leftover) chicken

1 (10-inch) flour tortilla

1/2 cup shredded romaine lettuce

1/3 cup shredded Mexican cheese

1/4 cup diced tomatoes

DIRECTIONS

1. In a small mixing bowl, combine the chipotle mayo with the cooked chicken.

2. Place this chicken and mayo mixture in the center of the tortilla.

3. Add the shredded romaine lettuce and Mexican cheese to the chicken mixture, then top with the tomatoes.

4. Begin wrapping the tortilla by folding one of the longer sides over the filling. Then, fold in both of the shorter sides over the initial fold.

5. Hold the filling tightly within the tortilla and continue rolling it until it's completely wrapped.

6. Heat a dry skillet, and add the wrap. Toast it for 2-3 minutes, turning once, until the wrap surface is slightly charred. Serve immediately.

FUN FACT

Chipotle chicken is like a secret flavor superhero. Chipotle peppers have a smoky and spicy kick, but they also have a bit of sweetness that makes them exciting but not too overwhelming. So, when you taste chipotle chicken, you're experiencing a delicious flavor adventure where the smoky superhero saves the day, making your meal both exciting and yummy!

COOKING FOR FRIENDS

Homemade Pizza

Servings: 4 | Prep + Cooking time: 1 hour 20 minutes

INGREDIENTS

3 1/2 cups all-purpose flour

1 teaspoon instant yeast

1 teaspoon salt

1 tablespoon olive oil, plus extra for drizzling

3 ounces tomato pizza sauce

For the topping:

1 4-ounce mozzarella ball, sliced

1 ounce grated Parmesan

2 ounces cherry tomatoes, halved

Cooked ham, sliced

Handful of basil leaves

DIRECTIONS

1. In a large bowl, combine the flour, yeast, and salt. Create a well in the center, and pour in 3/4 cup of warm water and the olive oil. Mix with a wooden spoon to form a soft, somewhat wet dough. Knead on a lightly floured surface for 5 minutes until smooth. Cover with a tea towel and set aside. Allow the dough to rise for about 1 hour.

2. When the dough has risen, knead it briefly, then divide it into two balls. On a floured surface, roll each ball into a round, roughly 10-inches in diameter. Aim for a very thin dough as it will puff up in the oven. Preheat the oven to 450°F.

3. Transfer the rounds onto two floured baking sheets or trays. Spread the sauce over each base, season to taste, then add mozzarella, Parmesan, tomatoes, and ham. Drizzle with olive oil. Place a baking sheet or tray the oven on the top shelf.

4. Bake each pizza for 8-12 minutes or until crisp. If desired, finish with a drizzle of olive oil and basil leaves. Repeat with the second pizza. Enjoy your delicious homemade pizzas with your friends or family.

Chicken Nuggets

Servings: 4 | Prep + Cooking time: 35 minutes

INGREDIENTS

2 boneless, skinless chicken breasts

1 cup all-purpose flour

2 eggs

2 tablespoons water

1 cup breadcrumbs

½ teaspoon smoked paprika

½ cup Parmesan cheese

1 tablespoon Italian seasoning

1 teaspoon garlic salt

Oil for frying

Ketchup and mayo to serve

DIRECTIONS

1. Cut the chicken breasts into bite-sized pieces, about 1 ½ inches each.

2. Place flour in one medium bowl. In a second bowl, beat the eggs and water together. Mix breadcrumbs, Parmesan cheese, Italian seasoning, garlic salt, and paprika in a third bowl.

3. Pour about 2 inches of oil into a frying pan and heat it over medium heat to 350°F.

4. As the oil heats, coat the chicken pieces by dredging them in flour, dipping them into the egg mixture, and finally coating them in the breadcrumb mixture.

5. Test the oil by adding one nugget. It should sizzle right away.

6. If it browns too quickly without cooking through, lower the heat.

7. Fry the nuggets in batches, cooking for 3–4 minutes on each side.

8. Drain them on a wire rack or a plate lined with paper towels before serving.

9. Enjoy your flavorful chicken nuggets with ketchup, mayonnaise, or any other sauce of your choice.

Tacos

Servings: 4 | Prep + Cooking time: 20 minutes

INGREDIENTS

½ pound ground beef

1 small onion, chopped

¼ teaspoon salt

1 (1-ounce) package taco seasoning

1 cup refried beans

¾ cup salsa

8 taco shells or warmed corn tortillas

1 cup shredded lettuce

1 cup shredded cheddar cheese

1 sliced avocado

1 diced tomato

DIRECTIONS

1. Warm a large frying pan over medium heat for 2 minutes.

2. Add the ground beef and chopped onion. Cook for about 5 minutes, stirring frequently to crumble the beef, until the onion becomes translucent. Drain any excess fat. Mix in the salt and taco seasoning.

3. Add the refried beans and salsa to the beef mixture.

4. Stir and cook for another 2 minutes or until everything is thoroughly heated.

5. Evenly distribute the beef mixture into the taco shells.

6. Top each taco with shredded lettuce, cheddar cheese, diced tomatoes, and sliced avocado.

7. Feel free to add any other desired toppings and enjoy your delicious tacos!

TIP

For chicken tacos, substitute the ground beef with 2 chicken breasts cut into bite-sized pieces.

Philadelphia Sushi Rolls

Servings: 4 | Prep + Cooking time: 30 minutes

INGREDIENTS

2 cups (1 pound) sushi rice, cooked

¼ cup (60 ml) seasoned rice vinegar

4 half sheets of sushi-grade nori

1 teaspoon sesame seeds

4 oz smoked salmon

4 oz firm cream cheese, cut into matchsticks

1 small cucumber, cut into matchsticks

Pickled ginger and wasabi for garnish

DIRECTIONS

1. Combine the sushi rice with the seasoned rice vinegar.

2. While mixing, fan the rice to bring it down to room temperature.

3. Place a nori sheet, rough side up, on a sushi rolling mat.

4. With wet hands, take a portion of rice and gently spread it across the nori sheet, ensuring an even layer without compressing the rice.

5. About 1 inch from the bottom edge of the nori, arrange a horizontal line of smoked salmon, cream cheese, and cucumber slices.

6. Carefully roll the mat from the bottom, enclosing the filling, and press gently to form a firm roll.

7. Continue pressing along the length of the roll to maintain its shape.

8. Move the sushi roll to a cutting board. Moisten a knife with a damp paper towel, then slice the roll into six even pieces.

9. Serve your delicious sushi rolls with pickled ginger and wasabi for an authentic touch.

Meatballs

Servings: 4 | Prep + Cooking time: 35 minutes

INGREDIENTS

1/4 cup breadcrumbs

1/4 cup Parmesan, grated

1/4 teaspoon of garlic powder

1/4 teaspoon of onion powder

1/4 teaspoon of Italian seasoning

1/8 teaspoon of salt

1/8 teaspoon of black pepper

1 large egg

1/8 cup of whole milk

1 pound of ground beef

1 tablespoon fresh parsley, chopped

DIRECTIONS

1. Preheat your oven to 400°F. Line a baking sheet with parchment paper.

2. Start by mixing the breadcrumbs, Parmesan, garlic, onion, Italian seasoning, salt, and pepper in a small bowl. In another small bowl, gently beat the egg.

3. In a large bowl, combine the breadcrumb mixture, beaten egg, milk, ground beef, and the freshly chopped parsley.

4. Mix everything with your hands until the ingredients are just combined, being careful not to overmix.

5. Let the mixture rest for about five minutes, which allows the breadcrumbs to absorb the moisture and soften.

6. Shape the mixture into approximately 16 meatballs, using about 2 tablespoons of mixture per meatball.

7. Place the meatballs on the baking sheet 1-inch apart from each other.

8. Bake for 17-20 minutes or until lightly browned.

9. Enjoy with spaghetti, tomato sauce or any other combination of your preference.

Chili Con Carne

Servings: 6 | Prep + Cooking time: 45 minutes

INGREDIENTS

1 tablespoon olive oil

3 garlic cloves, minced

1 onion, diced

1 red bell pepper, diced

1 lb ground beef

3 tablespoons tomato paste

1 can (28-ounce) crushed tomatoes

1 can (14-ounce) red kidney beans

2 cups beef broth

1 1/2 teaspoons sugar

1/2 cup water

Salt and pepper to taste

SPICE MIX:

2 teaspoons smoked paprika

2 teaspoons cumin powder

2 teaspoons onion powder

2 teaspoons oregano

DIRECTIONS

1. Heat olive oil in a large skillet over medium-high heat. Add garlic and onions, and cook for 1 minute. Add the red bell pepper and cook for 2 more minutes until the onion is translucent.

2. Increase heat to high and add ground beef.

3. Cook, breaking it apart, until it is mostly browned. Stir in the Spice Mix and continue cooking until the beef is fully browned.

4. Add the crushed tomatoes, beans, broth, sugar, and 1/2 cup of water. Bring to a simmer, then adjust the heat to medium-low.

5. Cook for 20 to 40 minutes, uncovered, so it gently bubbles. Before serving, adjust salt and pepper to taste.

6. Serve the chili over rice or in bowls accompanied by corn chips or warm tortillas. Add your favorite toppings, such as sour cream, cheese, and cilantro.

Tuna Quesadillas

Servings: 4 | Prep + Cooking time: 15 minutes

INGREDIENTS

10 ounces canned tuna chunks in spring water, drained

3 ounces canned sweet corn in water, drained

2 tablespoons mayonnaise

8 plain tortilla wraps

30 ounces cheddar cheese, grated

1 ounce baby spinach, chopped

4 teaspoons olive oil

DIRECTIONS

1. In a bowl, combine the drained tuna chunks, mayonnaise, and corn.

2. Season with black pepper to taste.

3. Place half of the tortilla wraps on a flat surface.

4. Spread the tuna mixture over these wraps, leaving a small border around the edges.

5. Sprinkle the grated cheese and chopped spinach evenly over the tuna mixture. Top each with another tortilla wrap to form a sandwich.

6. Heat 1 teaspoon of olive oil in a frying pan over medium-high heat.

7. Place one quesadilla in the pan and toast for 2-3 minutes on each side or until the tortillas are golden brown and the cheese has melted.

8. Add the remaining oil to the pan and repeat the process with the second quesadilla.

9. Transfer the cooked quesadillas to a cutting board and slice each into quarters.

10. Enjoy!

Mac 'n Cheese

Servings: 8 | Prep + Cooking time: 35 minutes

INGREDIENTS

1 pound of dried elbow pasta

1/2 cup unsalted butter

1/2 cup all-purpose flour

1 1/2 cups whole milk

2 1/2 cups half and half

4 cups cheddar cheese, shredded

2 cups Pepper Jack cheese, shredded

1/2 tablespoon salt

1/2 teaspoon black pepper

1/4 teaspoon smoked paprika

DIRECTIONS

1. Preheat your oven to 330°F. Grease a 9x13-inch baking dish (or similar) and set aside. Boil a large pot of salted water. Add dried pasta and cook for 1 minute less than the package instructions for al dente. Drain and toss with a bit of olive oil to prevent sticking.

2. While the water is heating, shred the cheddar cheese and Pepper Jack cheese and mix them. Divide into three parts: approximately 3 cups for the sauce, 1 1/2 cups for the inner layer, and 1 1/2 cups for the topping.

3. Melt butter over medium heat in a large saucepan. Add flour and whisk, cooking for about 1 minute until it resembles wet sand. Gradually pour in the half and half, whisking constantly until smooth. Then, slowly add the whole milk, whisk until smooth, and the mixture thickens significantly.

4. Remove from heat, stir in the salt, pepper, and paprika. Gradually add 3 cups of the mixed cheeses, stirring until completely melted and smooth.

5. Combine the drained pasta with the cheese sauce in a large mixing bowl, ensuring it's coated. Pour half of the pasta mixture into the prepared dish, layer with 1 1/2 cups of shredded cheese, then top with the remaining pasta mixture.

6. Sprinkle the remaining 1 1/2 cups of cheese on top and bake for 15 minutes or until the cheese is bubbly and lightly golden brown. Enjoy your creamy, flavorful mac and cheese!

Lasagna

Servings: 8 | Prep + Cooking time: 1 hour 40 minutes

INGREDIENTS

8-9 ounces of no-boil lasagna noodles

2 eggs, beaten

16 ounces of ricotta cheese

4 cups of shredded mozzarella cheese, divided

1/2 cup of Parmesan cheese

1 pound of ground beef, browned

5 cups of pasta sauce

1 cup of spinach, chopped

Parsley, for garnish

DIRECTIONS

1. Preheat your oven to 370°F.

2. In a bowl, mix together the beaten eggs, ricotta cheese, 2 cups of mozzarella cheese, and Parmesan cheese. Set aside.

3. Spread 1 cup of sauce on the bottom of a 13x9x3 inch baking pan.

4. Start layering with 4 uncooked lasagna noodles (they may overlap), followed by a third of the ricotta mixture, half of the browned meat, 1 cup of mozzarella, and 1 cup of sauce.

5. For the next layer, use 4 more uncooked noodles, another third of the ricotta mixture, the chopped spinach, and 1 1/2 cups of sauce.

6. The third layer includes 4 more noodles, the remaining ricotta mixture, the remaining meat, and 1 cup of sauce.

7. Finally, top with 4 noodles, the remaining sauce, and the last cup of mozzarella. Cover with foil and bake for 50-60 minutes.

8. Uncover and bake for another 5 minutes or until the cheese on top has melted.

9. Allow the lasagna to stand for 15 minutes before garnishing with parsley and serving.

No-Bake Cheese Ball

Servings: 8 | Prep + Cooking time: 20 minutes

INGREDIENTS

16 ounces cream cheese, at room temperature

1 1/2 cups of shredded cheddar cheese

1 teaspoon Worcestershire sauce

1 teaspoon ranch dressing mix

1 teaspoon garlic powder

1/2 cup almonds, crushed

1/4 cup chopped green onions

DIRECTIONS

1. Blend the cream cheese in a large bowl or using a stand mixer until smooth.

2. Add the cheddar cheese, ranch dressing mix, green onions, Worcestershire sauce, and garlic, and mix everything until it's thoroughly combined.

3. Spoon the cream cheese mixture onto a piece of foil or cling film.

4. Fold the edges of the foil or wrap it over and shape the mixture into a ball.

5. Ensure the ball is completely enclosed in the wrap.

6. Refrigerate the cheese ball for at least one hour to firm up.

7. After chilling, unwrap the cheese ball and press the crushed almonds all around the surface of the ball, ensuring they adhere well.

8. Serve this delightful cheese ball and enjoy its rich and flavorful taste!

TIP

In recent years, cheese balls have become a popular holiday tradition in many households. They're often shaped into festive forms like snowmen, pumpkins, or Christmas trees, making them a fun and decorative addition to holiday gatherings. So, during the holiday season, cheese balls not only delight your taste buds but also add a touch of edible artistry to your celebrations!

Tomato & Basil Bruschetta

Servings: 12 | Prep + Cooking time: 20 minutes

INGREDIENTS

1 small French baguette

3 medium ripe tomatoes. diced

1/4 cup basil leaves, chopped

2 tablespoons extra-virgin olive oil

1 garlic clove, minced

1/4 sea salt or to taste

1/4 cup finely chopped onion

Balsamic vinegar and flaky salt

DIRECTIONS

1. Preheat your oven to 450°F. Line a baking sheet with parchment paper.

2. In a mixing bowl, add the tomatoes and mix in the salt, onion, basil, and garlic. Set aside. Diagonally slice the baguette into pieces, each no thicker than 1/2-inch.

3. Lightly coat both sides of each slice with olive oil, about 1 tablespoon. Arrange the slices in a single layer on the baking sheet and bake them on the middle rack for 6-9 minutes or until they are crisp and golden brown on top.

4. Place them on 1-2 serving plates. Drain any excess juice from the tomato mixture using your hand to keep the solids in the bowl. Mix in the remaining olive oil.

5. Spoon the tomato mixture onto each toast, tilting your spoon to let any excess juice drip into the bowl. For a final touch, lightly drizzle thick balsamic vinegar over the top and sprinkle with flaky salt. Serve immediately.

FUN FACT

Its name comes from the Italian word "bruscare," which means "to roast over coals" or "to toast. The crispy, toasted bread serves as the perfect canvas for all kinds of colorful and tasty toppings, making bruschetta a creative and yummy treat. Plus, it's a great introduction to trying different ingredients and flavors, which can be an exciting culinary adventure for your taste buds!

Ham & Cheese Roll-ups

Servings: 16 | Prep + Cooking time: 8 hours

INGREDIENTS

4 ounces cream cheese, at room temperature

1/4 teaspoon garlic powder

1/2 cup shredded cheddar cheese

1 tablespoon dill pickle relish

2 (8-inch) tortilla shells

1/4 pound deli ham

1/4 cup finely chopped chives

DIRECTIONS

1. In a large mixing bowl, use a hand mixer to whip the cream cheese with garlic powder until it becomes light and fluffy.

2. Fold in the shredded cheddar cheese, pickle relish, and chives.

3. Evenly spread the cream cheese mixture over each tortilla shell, extending it to the edges.

4. Distribute the ham slices equally across the tortilla shells.

5. Tightly roll up the tortillas and wrap them securely in cling film. Refrigerate the rolls for 4 hours, or overnight, for best results.

6. Once chilled, remove the rolls from the refrigerator and unwrap them.

7. Trim off the edges for a clean look.

8. Cut each roll in half, then slice each half into smaller pieces, resulting in 8 roll-ups per tortilla.

9. Serve immediately or store in an airtight container in the fridge for up to two days.

10. Enjoy these delicious and convenient roll-ups as a snack or part of a meal.

Fajitas

Servings: 6 | Prep + Cooking time: 30 minutes

INGREDIENTS

3 chicken breasts

1 onion

1 lime

3 bell peppers, mixed colors

3 tablespoons olive oil, divided

1 teaspoon chili powder

1/2 teaspoon smoked paprika

1/2 teaspoon onion powder

1/2 teaspoon black pepper

1/4 cup cilantro, freshly chopped

Salt to taste

DIRECTIONS

1. Cut the onion into thin slivers and slice the bell peppers.

2. In a separate bowl, whisk together 1 tablespoon of olive oil, the juice from half a lime, chili powder, paprika, onion powder, black pepper, cumin, and salt. Slice the chicken breasts into strips and toss them in the spice mixture to coat well.

3. Heat 1 tablespoon of olive oil in a skillet over medium-high heat.

4. Cook the chicken strips for 3-5 minutes. Remove the cooked chicken from the skillet and set aside. Cook in two batches if needed.

5. After removing the chicken, add another tablespoon of oil to the pan.

6. Add the onions and cook for 2 minutes. Then, add the sliced bell peppers and cook for an additional 2 minutes or until they are just heated through.

7. Return the chicken to the pan with the vegetables. Stir everything together to combine.

8. Remove from the heat, squeeze the remaining lime juice, and sprinkle with the freshly chopped cilantro.

9. Serve the mixture over tortillas and top with your favorite topping.

Tater Tots

Servings: 6 | Prep + Cooking time: 45 minutes

INGREDIENTS

2 pounds of russet potatoes, peeled

1 tablespoon flour

1 teaspoon garlic powder

1/2 teaspoon onion powder

1/4 teaspoon dried oregano

1/4 teaspoon dried dill

Kosher salt and black pepper to taste

3 cups vegetable oil for frying

2 tablespoons parsley, chopped

1/4 cup grated Parmesan cheese

DIRECTIONS

1. Place the peeled potatoes in a Dutch oven and cover them with cold, salted water by one inch. Bring the water to a boil, lower the heat and let simmer, covered for about 7 minutes or until the potatoes are parboiled.

2. Drain them well and allow them to cool.

3. Finely shred the potatoes using a box grater.

4. Then, using a clean dish towel or cheesecloth, thoroughly drain the shredded potatoes, squeezing out as much water as possible.

5. Move the drained potatoes to a large bowl. Add in the flour, garlic, onion, oregano, dill, and grated Parmesan cheese.

6. Season the mixture with salt and pepper to taste. The mix should be manageable but dry. Shape the potatoes into tots.

7. Heat the vegetable oil in a large stockpot or Dutch oven over medium-high heat. The oil is ready for frying when it reaches 360°F on a deep-fry thermometer.

8. Fry the tots in batches, cooking each until evenly golden brown and crispy, about 3-4 minutes. After frying, transfer the tots to a plate lined with paper towels.

9. Serve the tots hot, garnished with chopped parsley and your favorite topping.

Nachos

Servings: 4 | Prep + Cooking time: 10 minutes

INGREDIENTS

1 cup canned black beans, drained and rinsed

1 bag of tortilla chips

1 cup salsa

2 tomatoes, diced

2 avocados, diced

1 jalapeño, sliced

1 cup shredded cheddar cheese

1 cup sour cream

DIRECTIONS

1. Arrange the tortilla chips in a single layer in a microwave-safe dish.

2. Layer the chips with black beans and shredded cheddar cheese blend.

3. Place the dish in the microwave and heat it for 1 minute or until the cheese has fully melted.

4. Top the nachos with salsa, tomatoes, avocadoes, and jalapeño slices.

5. Finish by dolloping the sour cream evenly over the nachos. Enjoy.

FUN FACT

Nachos were created by a Mexican named Ignacio "Nacho" Anaya in the 1940s. Legend has it that he quickly put together the dish when a group of U.S. military wives visited the restaurant he worked at, and he needed a snack to serve them. He improvised by melting cheese over tortilla chips and adding jalapeño peppers, creating what we now know as nachos.

Devilled Eggs

Servings: 6 | **Prep Time**: 10 minutes

INGREDIENTS

6 hard-boiled eggs, cold

6 tablespoons mayonnaise

3 teaspoons Dijon mustard

Salt and black pepper to taste

1/2 teaspoon sweet paprika

1 tablespoon parsley, chopped

DIRECTIONS

1. Peel the hard-boiled eggs and cut them in half lengthwise.

2. Gently scoop out the yolks and place them in a bowl.

3. Mash the yolks with a fork and mix in mayonnaise, Dijon mustard, salt, and pepper.

4. Spoon the yolk mixture back into the egg whites.

5. Sprinkle paprika over the top for a burst of color and flavor.

6. Top with parsley for a fresh touch.

TIP

Sprinkle some crispy bacon bits, finely chopped pickles, or grated cheese.

It's fun to personalize your deviled eggs and discover new flavor combinations!

Meatloaf

Servings: 6 | Prep + Cooking time: 1 hour 20 minutes

INGREDIENTS

1/2 onion, diced

1 teaspoon butter

2 eggs

3/4 cup milk

3/4 cup seasoned breadcrumbs

2 pounds lean ground beef

1 tablespoon BBQ sauce

1 teaspoon Italian seasoning

2 tablespoons parsley, freshly chopped

1 teaspoon Kosher salt + to taste

1/2 teaspoon black pepper + to taste

1/2 cup chili sauce

1/2 cup ketchup

DIRECTIONS

1. Preheat your oven to 360°F. Line a rimmed baking pan with aluminum foil and coat it lightly with cooking spray. In a small pan, gently cook the onions in butter over medium-low heat until they become tender. Allow them to cool completely.

2. In a medium-sized bowl, whisk together the eggs, milk, and breadcrumbs. Let this mixture sit for 5-10 minutes to soak.

3. Add the ground beef, the cooled cooked onions, BBQ sauce, Italian seasoning, parsley, and salt and pepper to the breadcrumb mixture. Combine everything until mixed.

4. Shape the mixture into an 8"x4" loaf on the prepared baking pan. Bake it for 40 minutes in the preheated oven.

5. Meanwhile, prepare the sauce by mixing the chili sauce and ketchup.

6. After 40 minutes of baking, spread this sauce over the meatloaf.

7. Return the meatloaf to the oven and bake it for another 10-15 minutes, or until cooked through and reaches an internal temperature of 160°F.

8. Let the meatloaf rest for 10 minutes before slicing and serving.

Carolina-Style Pulled Pork Sandwiches

Servings: 10 | Prep + Cooking time: 12 hours

INGREDIENTS

3 to 4 pounds pork shoulder

1/2 cup water, divided

28-ounces barbecue sauce

10 to 12 Kaiser rolls

FOR THE COLESLAW:

1 tablespoon sugar

1 tablespoon apple cider vinegar

1/4 teaspoon salt

1/2 cup mayonnaise

1 (14-ounce) package coleslaw mix

DIRECTIONS

1. The night before serving, place the pork shoulder in a slow cooker with 1/2 cup of water. Cover and cook on low for 10 to 12 hours.

2. In the morning, shred the cooked pork using a fork and return it to the slow cooker. Pour the barbecue sauce over the shredded pork and mix until everything is well combined.

3. Keep the mixture on low heat in the slow cooker until you're ready to serve. Serve the pork on Kaiser rolls or toasted hamburger buns.

4. For the coleslaw, in a small bowl, whisk together sugar, vinegar, and salt until the sugar and salt dissolve. Then, whisk in the mayonnaise until it's fully incorporated.

5. Place the coleslaw mix in a large mixing bowl. Pour the mayonnaise dressing over the coleslaw mix and toss until the coleslaw is evenly coated.

6. Serve this delicious barbecue pork topped with coleslaw, in true Southern style, or with coleslaw on the side.

Pigs in Blankets

Servings: 8 | Prep + Cooking time: 20 minutes

INGREDIENTS

1 (8-ounce) can of refrigerated crescent rolls

8 chicken sausages (instead of hot dogs)

1/4 cup of grated cheddar cheese

1 egg, lightly beaten

1 tablespoon water

Sesame seeds for topping

DIRECTIONS

1. Preheat your oven to 370° F. Lightly oil a baking sheet and put it aside.

2. Unroll the crescent dough and separate it into individual triangles. Sprinkle with cheddar cheese and place a chicken sausage at the wide end of each dough triangle.

3. Roll up towards the narrow end. Arrange these on the prepared baking sheet.

4. In a small bowl, whisk together the beaten egg and water to create an egg wash. Brush this mixture over the tops of the crescent-wrapped sausages.

5. Generously sprinkle sesame seeds over the rolls and press them in gently so they adhere.

6. Bake in the oven for 12-15 minutes or until the rolls turn a lovely golden brown.

FUN FACT

Pigs in blankets' history dates back to medieval England. Originally known as "sausage rolls" or "sausage in pastry," they were a popular dish at lavish feasts during the Tudor period. These early versions often featured spiced sausages wrapped in a flaky pastry. Over time, pigs in blankets made their way to America, where they became a beloved appetizer, especially during holiday gatherings.

Savory Muffins

Servings: 6 | Prep + Cooking time: 30 minutes

INGREDIENTS

4 ounces smoked deli ham, chopped

1/2 teaspoon oil

1 cup self-raising flour

1 teaspoon baking powder

1 egg

1 1/2 ounces butter, softened

100 ml milk

3 cherry tomatoes, halved

1 ounce grated Cheddar cheese

DIRECTIONS

1. Preheat your oven to 370°F.

2. Prepare a muffin tin by lining it with 6 paper cases.

3. In a frying pan, cook the deli ham in oil for about 5 minutes until crispy.

4. Allow it to cool, then mix it with the self-raising flour and baking powder.

5. In a separate bowl, whisk together the egg, butter, and milk.

6. Combine this mixture with the dry ingredients, stirring until just combined.

7. Divide the batter evenly among the prepared muffin cases.

8. Place a halved cherry tomato on top of each muffin and sprinkle with grated Cheddar cheese.

9. Bake in the oven for 18-20 minutes, until the muffins are golden brown.

10. Remove them from the oven and let them cool.

TIP

As a snack, serve it with carrot sticks, fried edamame, and/or pineapple fingers.

DESSERTS

Banana Cupcakes

Servings: 6 | Prep + Cooking time: 30 minutes

INGREDIENTS

Cooking spray

¾ cup flour

2 tablespoons melted butter

¼ teaspoon baking soda

¼ teaspoon baking powder

¼ teaspoon salt

2 ripe bananas, divided

¼ cup sugar

1 egg

2 tablespoons vegetable oil

1 ½ teaspoons vanilla extract

DIRECTIONS

1. Preheat your oven to 360°F. Coat 6 remekins with cooking spray.

2. In a bowl, mix together the flour, butter, baking soda, and baking powder. Set aside.

3. In a different bowl, thoroughly mash 1 ½ bananas. Stir in sugar, salt, oil, egg, and vanilla extract until well combined. Gradually add the flour mixture to the banana mixture, whisking constantly to ensure a smooth batter.

4. Pour the batter into the ramekins, filling each three-quarters full. Slice the remaining ½ of banana thinly and top each muffin with 2-3 slices.

5. Bake for 15-17 minutes, or until a toothpick inserted into the center of one cupcake comes out clean.

TIP

If you want to use berries, substitute the bananas with one cup of fresh or frozen berries, but add them all when mixing the batter.

Peanut Butter Brownies

Servings: 4 | Prep + Cooking time: 35 minutes

INGREDIENTS

Nonstick cooking spray

1 cup peanut butter

2 eggs

¾ cup flour

DIRECTIONS

1. Preheat your oven to 360°F. Lightly coat an 8-by-8-inch baking pan with cooking spray.

2. In a medium-sized bowl, blend peanut butter, eggs, and flour until it forms a glossy, dense batter, ensuring it's free of lumps.

3. Transfer this batter to your greased pan.

4. Place the pan in the middle of the oven and bake for 18-20 minutes or until a toothpick poked in the center emerges without any batter sticking to it.

5. Let it cool a bit, and cut into 4 brownies. Enjoy!

TIP

For extra sweetness, dust with powdered sugar or spread chocolate frosting over.

Nutty Energy Balls

Servings: 12 balls | **Prep Time**: 10 minutes + chilling time

INGREDIENTS

1 tablespoon brown sugar

¼ cup almond butter

2 tablespoons chopped almonds

2 tablespoons sunflower seeds

½ cup chopped dried cranberries

½ cup chopped dark chocolate

DIRECTIONS

1. Place the brown sugar, almond butter, and salt in a small microwave-safe bowl and microwave for 30 seconds on high.

2. Remove and stir the mixture and return to the microwave.

3. Microwave for another 30 seconds on high or until the mixture is hot and the brown sugar is dissolved.

4. Stir well with the nuts, cranberries, and chocolate chips in a mixing bowl.

5. Carefully pour the hot almond butter mixture over the nut mixture.

6. Stir with a spatula to combine, allowing the heat to melt the chocolate.

7. Shape the mixture into 1-inch balls, packing them with your hands.

8. Arrange the balls on a baking sheet and refrigerate them until set, approximately 2 hours.

9. Store the balls in a covered container in the refrigerator.

TIP

For extra sweetness, add mashed ripe bananas along with the nuts, cranberries and choco chips. If almonds are not your favorite nuts, substitute them for pecans or hazelnuts.

Chocolate Chip & Cinnamon Cookies

Servings: 10-12 | Prep + Cooking time: 25 minutes

INGREDIENTS

2 ½ cups flour

1 teaspoon baking soda

1 teaspoon salt

1 cup unsalted butter, softened

¾ cup sugar

1 teaspoon cinnamon

¾ cup light brown sugar

1 teaspoon vanilla extract

2 large eggs

2 cups semisweet chocolate chips

DIRECTIONS

1. Preheat your oven to 360°F.

2. In a mixing bowl, sift together the flour, baking soda, and salt.

3. In another bowl, mix the butter, sugar, brown sugar, cinnamon, and vanilla extract.

4. Add the eggs one at a time, thoroughly mixing after each addition.

5. Gradually add the flour mixture in three parts, mixing just enough to blend each time. Fold in the dark chocolate chunks.

6. Drop the dough in tablespoon-sized scoops onto ungreased baking sheets.

7. Bake them in the oven until golden, about 10-12 minutes.

8. Allow the cookies to cool slightly on the pans before moving them to a wire rack to cool completely.

Oatmeal Raisin Cookies

Servings: 14-16 cookies | Prep + Cooking time: 45 minutes

INGREDIENTS

½ cup unsalted butter, softened, plus extra for greasing

½ cup light brown sugar, packed

¼ cup granulated sugar

2 small eggs

1 teaspoon vanilla extract

¾ cup flour

¼ teaspoon salt

1 teaspoon baking soda

½ teaspoon ground cinnamon

¼ teaspoon ground nutmeg

1 ½ cups rolled oats

¾ cup raisins

DIRECTIONS

1. Preheat your oven to 360°F. Grease a large cookie sheet with butter.

2. Cream the butter in a bowl using an electric mixer until smooth.

3. Add brown and granulated sugars, beating until the mixture is fluffy for about 2 minutes. Incorporate the eggs one at a time, followed by the vanilla extract.

4. In a separate bowl, combine the flour, salt, baking soda, cinnamon, and nutmeg using a wooden spoon or spatula.

5. On low speed, gradually add this dry mixture to the butter mixture. Stir in the oats and raisins.

6. Drop the dough in tablespoonfuls onto the prepared cookie sheet, spacing them at least 2 inches apart.

7. Bake until the edges of the cookies are golden brown, about 10-14 minutes.

8. The centers will remain soft but will firm up as they cool.

9. Allow the cookies to cool completely on a wire rack before storing them in an airtight container at room temperature.

Baked Apples

Servings: 4 | Prep + Cooking time: 1 hour 15 minutes

INGREDIENTS

4 granny smith apples

½ cup sugar

1 teaspoon ground cinnamon

½ teaspoon fresh grated ginger

Pinch of nutmeg

2 tablespoons cornstarch

2 tablespoons water

Pinch of salt

DIRECTIONS

1. Preheat your oven to 360°F. Prepare a 9×13-inch baking dish.

2. Peel the apples, remove their cores, quarter them, and slice them thinly lengthwise, aiming for consistency in thickness for even cooking.

3. Place the apple slices in the baking dish. In a small bowl, mix sugar, cinnamon, ginger, nutmeg, cornstarch, water, and salt.

4. Toss everything together to mix well. Sprinkle the apples with the mixture and toss to coat. Cover the dish loosely with foil.

5. Bake in the preheated oven for 40 minutes with the foil on.

6. Then, carefully remove the foil and continue baking for an additional 8-13 minutes, or until the apples are tender and have a slight caramelization.

7. Serve cooled and enjoy.

FUN FACT

In medieval Europe, baked apples were a popular treat during the fall and winter months. They were often stuffed with ingredients like cinnamon, sugar, and nuts before being baked. Not only did they provide a warm and sweet dessert, but they also filled homes with a delightful aroma.

Lemon Curd

Servings: 1 | Prep + Cooking time: 15 minutes

INGREDIENTS

3 tablespoons butter

1/3 cup granulated sugar

1 large egg

1 teaspoon lemon zest

1/3 cup lemon juice

1/3 teaspoon vanilla extract

1 pinch of sea salt

DIRECTIONS

1. In a small microwave-safe bowl, melt the butter in the microwave in 30-second bursts on high.

2. Then mix in the sugar, egg, zest, juice, vanilla and salt, whisking until the mixture is smooth.

3. Microwave on high for 1 minute, then stir. Microwave for another minute, then let it rest in the microwave for 2 minutes before whisking again.

4. Microwave the mixture for an additional 30 seconds.

5. Allow it to stand for 3 minutes, then whisk it once more.

6. Use a spoon to create a "ditch" in the curd.

7. If the ditch fills back in, microwave the mixture for another 30 seconds, let it stand for 2 minutes, and test again. The curd is ready when the ditch stays in place.

8. Transfer the curd to an airtight container and refrigerate. Use within 5 days.

TIP

To make it a lemon mousse, fold 3/4 cup lemon curd into 3/4 cup whipped cream. Place 1/4 cup curd in the bottom of a mason jar, spoon in the curd-and-whipped-cream mixture, and top with 1/4 cup whipped cream. Garnish with homemade cookies.

Apple Crumble Pie

Servings: 8 | Prep + Cooking time: 35 minutes

INGREDIENTS

1 (21-ounce) can apple pie filling

3⁄4 cup brown sugar

1 teaspoon cinnamon

1⁄4 teaspoon nutmeg

1⁄2 cup flour

1⁄2 cup oatmeal

1⁄3 cup butter, melted

DIRECTIONS

1. Start by preheating your oven to 400°F. Mix the apple pie filling into a 1 1/2-quart casserole dish.

2. In a medium-sized bowl, mix together the sugar, cinnamon, nutmeg, flour, and oatmeal.

3. Add the melted butter to this mixture, stirring until you get a crumbly texture.

4. Then, evenly distribute these crumbs over the pie filling.

5. Place the dish in the oven and bake for about 15–20 minutes, or until you see the pie filling bubbling and the crumb mixture turns golden brown.

6. Serve it warm for a delicious treat.

FUN FACT

In the United States, apple pie is often referred to as the "All-American Pie." It became a symbol of American patriotism, and the phrase "as American as apple pie" is commonly used to describe something quintessentially American. This association grew during World War II when soldiers would reply "Mom and apple pie" when asked what they were fighting for. So, beyond its delicious taste, apple pie represents a slice of the American history and culture.!

New York Cheesecake

Servings: 12 | Prep + Cooking time: 2 hours

INGREDIENTS

FOR THE CRUST:

1 1/2 cups graham cracker crumbs

1/4 cup sugar

1/2 cup unsalted butter, melted

FOR THE FILLING:

4 (8-ounce) packages cream cheese, softened

1 1/4 cups sugar

1 cup sour cream

2 teaspoons vanilla extract

4 large eggs

FOR THE TOPPING:

1 cup sour cream

2 tablespoons sugar

1 teaspoon vanilla extract

DIRECTIONS

1. Preheat your oven to 325°F. Mix the graham cracker crumbs, sugar, and melted butter until well combined.

2. Press the mixture into the bottom of a 9-inch springform pan.

3. Bake for 10 minutes, then remove from the oven and let it cool.

4. Meanwhile, in a large bowl, beat the cream cheese and sugar together until smooth. Mix in the sour cream and vanilla extract.

5. Add the eggs one at a time, beating until blended after each addition.

6. Pour the filling over the crust in the springform pan.

7. Bake for 1 hour and 10 minutes or until the center is almost set, and the top appears dull.

8. Remove the cheesecake from the oven and let it cool in the pan on a wire rack for 10 minutes. Carefully run a knife around the rim of the pan to loosen the cheesecake, then cool for another hour.

9. Mix 1 cup sour cream, 2 tablespoons sugar, and 1 teaspoon vanilla. Spread this mixture over the top of the cooled cheesecake.

10. Return the cheesecake to the oven and bake for an additional 10 minutes. Remove the cheesecake from the oven and cool completely on a wire rack. Refrigerate the cheesecake for at least 4 hours or overnight.

11. When ready to serve, remove the sides of the springform pan. Slice the cheesecake with a sharp, thin-bladed knife, dipping the knife in warm water and wiping it dry between each cut.

Yogurt & Raspberry Parfait

Servings: 1 | Prep + Cooking time: 10 minutes

INGREDIENTS

1 cup Greek yogurt

¾ cup raspberries

¼ cup granola

1 tablespoon chopped hazelnuts

1 teaspoon honey

DIRECTIONS

1. Take a 10-ounce mason jar and layer half of the Greek yogurt at the bottom. Follow with a layer of half the mixed berries and half the granola and hazelnuts.

2. Repeat the layers with the remaining yogurt, berries, granola, and hazelnuts. Seal the jar with its lid, and you're ready to take it to classes.

TIP

If you want to turn this into a true home served dessert, add a dollop of Homemade Whipped Cream and some chocolate chips.

Homemade Whipped Cream

Servings: 1 small bowl | Prep + Cooking time: 15 minutes

INGREDIENTS

1 cup heavy whipping cream

1 tablespoon powdered sugar

1 teaspoon vanilla extract

1/2 teaspoon lemon zest

DIRECTIONS

1. In a large bowl, combine the heavy cream, sugar, vanilla, and lemon zest.

2. Using an electric mixer, set it to medium speed to whip the mixture until you achieve medium peaks, which should take about 4 minutes.

3. Be careful not to over-whip, as this will turn your mixture into butter.

4. This whipped cream is best enjoyed soon, as it lasts only a day or two in the fridge.

TIP

For the best results, ensure your cream is cold.

Chilling a stainless-steel bowl in the freezer for 15 to 30 minutes before whipping can help achieve lighter whipped cream.

To create different flavors, you can substitute vanilla extract with almond extract or other flavored syrups.

FUN FACT

Whipped cream was a favorite treat among European nobility in the 16th century. At lavish banquets and royal feasts, it was common to have bowls of freshly whipped cream, and it was often flavored with ingredients like sugar and spices. Whipped cream was considered a symbol of luxury and indulgence, and it's still a beloved topping for desserts and beverages today!

S'Mores

Servings: 2 | Prep + Cooking time: 15 minutes

INGREDIENTS

2 Graham Crackers broken in half

2 marshmallows broken in half

2 small pieces (bars) dark chocolate

DIRECTIONS FOR AIR FRIED S'MORES

Arrange the crackers halves in the base of the Air Fryer.

Press the cut, sticky side of a marshmallow onto each Graham cracker, ensuring it adheres.

Secure the Air Fryer lid and set it to cook at 390°F for 5-7 minutes, or until the marshmallows turn a delightful golden hue.

After cooking, place a piece of chocolate on top of each marshmallow, then cap it with the remaining Graham cracker halves. Ready to be enjoyed.

DIRECTIONS FOR BAKED S'MORES

Preheat your oven to 360°F for 10 minutes.

Line a parchment paper on a baking tray and arrange the crackers. Place the chocolate bars, followed by the marshmallows.

Make sure there is enough space for it to bloom while baking.

Bake for 3-5 minutes, but keep an eye on them until the marshmallows are bloomed, and when they start to brown on top, remove the tray from the oven.

Seal with another cracker, press slightly. Now your baked s'mores are ready to serve!

Blueberry Cobbler

Servings: 6 | Prep + Cooking time: 40 minutes

INGREDIENTS

1 (21-ounce) can blueberry pie filling

½ cup flour

½ cup brown sugar

½ cup oatmeal

½ cup chopped pecans

½ teaspoon cinnamon

¼ cup butter, melted

DIRECTIONS

1. Preheat your oven to 400°F.

2. Pour the blueberry pie filling into a 9-inch square glass baking dish and set it aside.

3. In a medium bowl, mix together the flour, sugar, oatmeal, pecans, and cinnamon until well combined.

4. Drizzle the melted butter over this mixture and stir until it becomes crumbly.

5. Evenly sprinkle this crumbly mixture over the blueberry pie filling.

6. Bake in the oven for 20–25 minutes or until the pie filling is bubbly and the topping turns a light golden brown.

7. Serve warm, ideally with a scoop of ice cream or a dollop of whipped cream. Enjoy!

TIP

Sprinkle a small amount of lemon zest over the blueberry filling before adding the filling. The hint of citrusy brightness from the lemon zest complements the sweetness of the blueberries and adds a refreshing twist to the dessert. It's a simple addition that can elevate the flavor of your cobbler.

Snickerdoodle Cookie

Servings: 8 | Prep + Cooking time: 45 minutes

INGREDIENTS

½ cup granulated sugar, plus extra for topping

Nonstick cooking spray

½ cup packed brown sugar

¼ cup butter, melted

1 tablespoon pumpkin pie spice, plus extra for topping

1 large egg

1 teaspoon vanilla extract

1 cup plain flour

¼ teaspoon baking soda

DIRECTIONS

1. Preheat your oven to 380°F. Coat a 10-inch oven-safe skillet with nonstick cooking spray.

2. In a large mixing bowl, combine the brown sugar, granulated sugar, melted butter, and pumpkin pie spice. Mix until the mixture is smooth and free of large lumps.

3. Incorporate the egg and almond extract into the sugar mixture.

4. Next, add the flour and baking soda, stirring until a thick dough is formed. You may use your hands for the final mix to ensure thorough blending.

5. Firmly press this dough into the prepared skillet. Bake the cookie in the skillet for 20 minutes, or until the edges turn golden brown and the center is cooked. Let the cookie cool for 15 to 20 minutes.

6. You can slice the cookie while it's still in the skillet, or turn the skillet over to release the cookie and then cut it into 8 wedges.

7. Store the cookie wrapped in plastic or beeswax wrap in an airtight container at room temperature. It will keep well for up to a week.

Oreo Cheesecake

Servings: 10 | Prep + Cooking time: 12 hours

INGREDIENTS

24 Oreos, whole

16 Oreos, chopped

12 to 14 mini Oreos, chopped

4 tablespoons unsalted butter, melted

16 ounces cream cheese, softened

1 cup powdered sugar

1 teaspoon vanilla extract

2 cups cold heavy whipping cream

DIRECTIONS

1. Process the 24 oreos in a food processor until you have fine crumbs. Transfer the crumbs to a mixing bowl, and mix with the melted butter, until the crumbs are well moistened.

2. Line a 9-inch springform pan with parchment paper, transfer the crust mixture into the pan, and press it down firmly into an even layer. Place it in the refrigerator to chill while preparing the cheesecake filling.

3. Meanwhile, in a stand mixer with a whisk attachment or using a handheld mixer in a large bowl, beat the cream cheese until smooth. Add in the powdered sugar and vanilla extract, mixing until thoroughly combined.

4. In a separate bowl, whip the heavy cream. Start on low speed and gradually increase to medium-high, whipping until the cream thickens and stiff peaks form. Gently fold the whipped cream into the cream cheese mixture or blend on low speed until just combined. Then, fold in the 16 chopped Oreos.

5. Take the springform pan out of the refrigerator, add the cheesecake filling over the crust, and spread it evenly.

6. Cover the pan tightly and put it back in the refrigerator to chill for at least 8 hours.

7. Once set, remove the cheesecake from the pan, slice, and enjoy your delicious dessert!

Choco Fudge

Servings: 8-10 | Prep + Cooking time: 25 minutes

INGREDIENTS

1 tablespoon unsalted butter, to grease

1 ½ cups semisweet chocolate chips

½ cup milk chocolate chips

1 ¾ cups sweetened condensed milk

1 teaspoon orange zest (optional)

1 cup miniature marshmallows

1 teaspoon vanilla extract

DIRECTIONS

1. Start by greasing an 8" square baking pan with butter and set it aside.

2. In a medium, microwave-safe bowl, mix together the semisweet chocolate chips, milk chocolate chips, and condensed milk.

3. Microwave this mixture at medium power for 2–4 minutes, stirring halfway through, until the chocolate nearly melts.

4. Take the bowl out of the microwave and stir until the chocolate melts.

5. Stir in the miniature marshmallows.

6. To enhance the flavor, add the vanilla extract and the zest if using, and mix well.

7. Spread the mixture evenly into the prepared pan.

8. Allow it to stand at room temperature until it cools and sets.

9. Use a large, sharp knife to cut into squares, carefully wiping chocolate from the knife blade between cuts for a smooth cut.

10. Enjoy your delicious homemade treat!

Waffles

Servings: 3 | Prep + Cooking time: 25 minutes

INGREDIENTS

1 cup flour

1 teaspoon baking powder

¼ teaspoon salt

1 tablespoon sugar

2 eggs yolks

2 eggs whites

1 cup milk

¼ cup melted butter

1 teaspoon vanilla extract

Nonstick cooking spray

Cold butter to serve

Maple syrup to taste

DIRECTIONS

1. Preheat your waffle iron to 400°F.

2. In a large mixing bowl, whisk the flour, baking powder, sugar, and salt.

3. In a smaller bowl, blend together the egg yolks, milk, butter, and vanilla. Set aside.

4. In another medium-sized bowl, use a mixer at medium-high speed to whip the egg whites until they form stiff peaks.

5. Mix the wet egg yolk mixture into the bowl of dry ingredients, stirring until they're just combined.

6. Carefully fold in the whipped egg whites.

7. Grease the waffle iron with cooking spray and spoon the batter generously, making sure to cover most of the wells.

8. Shut the waffle iron and let the waffles cook for 3-5 minutes or until they turn a lovely golden brown.

9. Top them with butter and maple syrup, and enjoy your freshly made waffles!

Gooey Butter Cake

Servings: 10 | Prep + Cooking time: 60 minutes

INGREDIENTS

3 cups powdered sugar + some more for sprinkling 1 (15.25-ounce) box yellow cake mix

1 egg

½ cup butter, melted

1 cup cream cheese

2 eggs, beaten

1 teaspoon vanilla extract

½ teaspoon lemon zest

DIRECTIONS

1. Preheat your oven to 360°F and grease a 9x13-inch baking pan.

2. In a mixing bowl, combine the cake mix, one egg, and melted butter.

3. Blend until the mixture is smooth.

4. Press this mixture evenly into the bottom of your greased pan.

5. In another bowl, mix the cream cheese, 2 beaten eggs, vanilla extract, lemon zest, and powdered sugar until creamy and smooth.

6. Spread the cream cheese mixture over the cake mix layer in the pan.

7. Bake in the oven for 40-45 minutes or until the edges turn golden brown. The center might dip slightly.

8. Once baked, let it cool a bit, then sprinkle the top with additional powdered sugar.

9. Cut into 10 slices and enjoy your delicious treat!

Molten Lava Cakes

Servings: 4 | Prep + Cooking time: 40 minutes

INGREDIENTS

4 ounces unsalted butter, plus more for greasing the ramekins

6 ounces bittersweet chocolate, preferably Valrhona

2 eggs

2 egg yolks

1/4 cup sugar

1/2 teaspoon vanilla extract

Pinch of kosher salt

2 tablespoons flour, plus more for dusting the ramekins

Powdered sugar to dust

DIRECTIONS

1. Preheat your oven to 450°F. Apply butter to the insides of four 6-ounce ramekins and dust them lightly with flour, shaking out any excess. Place these ramekins on a baking tray.

2. Using a double boiler, gently melt the butter and chocolate together over simmering water.

3. In a separate bowl, using an electric mixer, vigorously whisk together the eggs, egg yolks, sugar, and salt on high speed until the mixture becomes thick and turns a lighter shade.

4. Ensure the melted chocolate is smooth, then swiftly fold it into the egg mixture, adding the flour. Divide this batter evenly among the prepared ramekins.

5. Bake in the preheated oven for 10-11 minutes. The cakes should be set around the edges but soft in the center. After baking, allow them to cool in the ramekins for a minute.

6. Next, place a dessert plate upside down on top of each ramekin. Carefully invert each cake onto the plate, wait for 10 seconds, then lift off the ramekin.

7. Dust with powdered sugar, pump it open, and serve.

TIP

A double boiler is a useful cooking technique. Grab a large pot, fill it with 2 inches of water, and bring it to a simmer. Place a smaller (glass) heatproof bowl that fits on top of the larger one without touching the water. Add your ingredients to the top bowl and cook gently, stirring as needed.

Cherry Pie

Servings: 6 | Prep + Cooking time: 1 hour

INGREDIENTS

1 1/2 cups fresh sweet cherries, pitted or canned cherries, drained

1/2 cup granulated sugar, plus 2 tablespoons for topping

3 large eggs, at room temperature   1/4 teaspoon salt

1/2 cup flour   Zest of 1 lemon

1 cup whole milk   Powdered sugar for dusting

1 1/2 teaspoons vanilla extract

DIRECTIONS

Preheat your oven to 360° F.

Generously butter the bottom of a 9-inch round baking dish.

Arrange the cherries evenly on the bottom of the prepared dish.

In a blender, combine the eggs, sugar, milk, flour, vanilla extract, salt, and lemon zest.

Blend until the mixture is smooth. Pour this batter over the cherries in the dish. Sprinkle the top with the 2 tablespoons of sugar.

Bake in the preheated oven for about 35-45 minutes or until the pie is set.

The crumble pie can be enjoyed warm, at room temperature, or chilled.

Made in the USA
Coppell, TX
19 December 2023

26616040R00061